HAUTE PURSUIT

A True Tale of Fashion, Fortune
& Fierce Ambition in New York City

Angela Taylor George

L

LUDLOW
PRESS

This memoir is a truthful recollection of events in the author's life.

This book may be purchased in bulk for promotional, educational, or business use. For information please email: buyme@ludlowpress.com

First Edition September 2023

Book Design by Hanna Day-Tenerowicz
Author Photo by Teige Alexandra
Model Photos by Della Bass and Takahiro Ogawa
Other photographs courtesy of the author

ISBN 979-8-9883163-0-5 (ebook)
ISBN 979-8-9883163-2-9 (paperback)
ISBN 979-8-9883163-1-2 (paperback)
ISBN 979-8-9883163-3-6 (hardcover)

To Mom,

Your strength and determination
live inside of me today.
I miss you dearly.

Contents

Introduction

t's one of the world's most dynamic cultural epicenters, where fashion rules and many of the hottest trends are born. A cutthroat place, it's home to a fiercely competitive industry that's dog-eat-dog, where intellectual property can barely be protected, and naïve designers can lose their names in a heartbeat. Welcome to New York City, my home and the place where I've made my fortune in fashion.

Sinatra said it best when he sang, "If I can make it there, I'll make it anywhere." And I did. Make no mistake, though, it wasn't all lollipops and rainbows. Far from it, in fact. There was intense pressure and heavy personal hardship along the way. But, looking back now, all that may have been the fuel to my fire. With relentless effort, undying passion, laser focus and a sprinkling of fairy dust luck, I persevered in my hot pursuit of reaching the top of my game.

My career has taken me from the retail selling floor to store leadership, from buyer to wholesale showroom founder, from designer to creative director and CEO of my own fashion brand. A full 360. I've seen it all in fashion commerce. Herein lies my story, my unique experience and what I've found to be invaluable along the way.

While you may think it's all glitz and glam, it's an industry that rewards exceptional talent, innovative thinking, and hard work. A true designer or aspiring fashion supernova of any kind has no choice but to eat, sleep, drink, and breathe this business. Trust me. The well-respected, aspirational brands at the top are not phoning it in. The front-facing flash you see is backed by not-so-glamorous hustle and grind. Oh, and schlepping, too, lots of it.

For those of you that are purely fashion-obsessed, get ready, because you're about to get a front row seat as I pull back the curtain to reveal how it all begins with a creative idea and winds up in your closet, highlighting each of the stages along the way. I'll even give you tasty bites of each decade, with pop references I experienced firsthand.

And for you mavericks who have dreams of being an entrepreneur or influencing fashion in some way, shape, or form, I'm living proof that all things are possible if you set your mind to it, believe in yourself, and are willing to do what it takes. Revealing my deep industry insights along the way, I'll leave it all on the stage, with the vital truths you need to know. If you absorb and apply even a fraction of the lessons nestled in the coming pages, your likelihood of success will be dramatically greater than that of your peers. I'm passing the baton, because perhaps it's your turn to build a fortune in fashion.

So, join me, fashion lovers and fortune seekers alike, as I take you through the decades and behind the scenes of one of the most highly coveted industries in the world. Let's go!

Yours truly, sashaying across the
hearth, belting out at the top of my lungs,
"I'm goin' to Hollywood!"

In the Beginning...

I had my first major fashion fix at age ten. It was 1970, and hit songs like The Beatles' "Let It Be" and "ABC" by The Jackson 5 were rocking the radio airwaves. Yes, no streaming back then and not even a thousand songs in your pocket. Don't remember the iPod? That's ok, too.

I spotted them out of the corner of my eye. The rack was overflowing with all different colors and patterns. I immediately locked in on the patriotic-looking ones. That was it. I swiftly ran home to get five bucks from my dad to score my very first pair of hot pants. That equals about fifty bucks today.

Those red, white, and blue striped twill short shorts with a front fly that showcased exposed decorative buttons were mine for the taking. Today, they're called booty shorts. The only difference is that back then, our cheeks didn't show. We were slightly more modest. Juuust slightly.

I grew up in a Long Island suburb of New York City. One of the Five Towns, Cedarhurst had a vibrant shopping village within walking distance from my house. Stores, packed, one after another, lined long streets extending as far as the eye could see. Everyone called it "town." "I'm going into town," we'd say.

Shopping was a big part of my youth. Even as a preschooler, I remember the elation I felt when they boxed up my old shoes, and I marched out of Stride Rite wearing my brand new ones. Or the time I got my first pair of white go-go boots that I flaunted in my first-grade graduation picture. Yeah, that's me beaming in the front on the left.

Then, there were the patent leather three-quarter high ones with the gold chains on the vamp. That's the front upper part. Purchased at Mays department store, I rocked those mod babies into third grade in two different colors, black and bone.

The earliest clothing store I shopped in was called Sisteen. That's where the hot pants were from, in case you were wondering. All the latest trends lined the massive walls and were stuffed into the maze of floor racks. There, they would throw you into a community fitting room. Okay, not actually throw, but you get the point. And the salesperson would scour the store and bring you a curated selection to try on.

One by one, pieces were tossed onto yes-and-no piles as she ran back and forth, bringing a seemingly endless stream of garments. I happily remember standing with my mom or big sister, Maria, by the checkout counter with glee as they neatly folded and bagged my new wardrobe stash.

In my teens, Huck-A-Poo and Wayne Rogers defined the times with their disco style. So culturally relevant,

Huck-a-Poo can be found today in The Costume Institute at the MET. These were buttoned-up pointy-collared shirts that came in a variety of bold geometric and conversational prints. And we intuitively started to collect them.

The idea was to acquire several in your wardrobe. And I set out to do just that, for they held status among my peers. From clothing to Cadillacs, The Five Towns was all about just that, status.

Eventually, a tiny store called Infinity opened on a side street off the main drag, Central Avenue. I would go in for the first time to find Holly, the owner, sitting cross-legged on the sky blue wall-to-wall shag carpet alongside brown shipping cartons. She seemed so fun and cool with her hip-hugger jeans and raspy voice.

Her enthusiasm was palpable as she dug in and tossed the clothes about on the rug. Fresh new merch. The skyrocketing anticipation of discovering what was in those boxes was a feeling that would follow me throughout my entire career and remains to this day.

I snagged my first Faded Glory two-piece sets that afternoon. Yes, plural, which might be a theme for me. I got the silver-studded, brushed twill jacket and pants in powder blue and peach. You know I'd later rock them with some '70s platforms.

Another must-stop shop was Ronnie's, with its corner location and mod, metallic silver façade that seemed to lure you in. Much bigger and louder, it was the opposite of Infinity. Ronnie, with his big, curly hair, was always behind the counter shouting things to his staff like, "Can you get me this in a size 7?" In those days, sizes for juniors were in odd numbers, and even numbers were for missy.

Then, there was Toulouse, the trendy fashion-forward shoe store. I'd buy my first pair of crepe chunky-heeled platform shoes in canvas multi-color checker plaid. Think Elton John, circa 1975. Kind of like that. Oh, and I'll never forget the brushed chambray high platforms I snagged with silver-studded peep toes. Très chic.

I remember another favorite shoe store in town called Jildor, where fellow Five Towns resident, Steve Madden, cut his teeth, in fact. When you asked to see a pair or two, they'd sit you down and have you place your foot in this silver, metal contraption that checked length and width. Then, they'd quickly disappear and come back with the ones you chose and a few more pairs you didn't ask to see. It worked. The art of the upsell. I'd often find myself walking out with styles I didn't even notice on the display. Now, they were merchants.

Thirteen Candles

Shopping back then was also a group sport meant to be shared with family and friends. We'd make a whole day of it. I'd hang out in town with my besties, meandering from store to store and hitting Mother Kelly's for lunch. Two slices and a Coke. We never talked about how Kelly was an Irish name for an Italian pizzeria, which only now dawns on me as I write this. Or, we'd end up at Pies Plus, a vibrant eatery in the center of town with harsh acoustics, made worse by the clatter of plates and utensils and loud Long Islanders ordering diet platters of tuna or cottage cheese and jello with flip top cans of Tab soda.

As an adolescent, a typical Saturday might look like this... First, we'd go to the stationer, Pik-a-Pak, and then over to the candle shop. It was the early '70s after all, a time of mood rings and puka shell chokers, and scents were everywhere. Heavily perfumed, decorative papers and cards to send our handwritten letters on and multi-colored, sweet-smelling candles, some looking like ice cream sundaes. And, of course, there was the incense we burned. Mmm, patchouli, my fave.

We'd hit Platterpuss for our vinyl tunes. There I scored my first albums, Seals & Crofts' Summer Breeze and Cat Stevens' Catch Bull At Four, which I played in my bedroom over and over... and over. Then, we'd hang out in front of Robert's, the beauty drug store and wait to see the cute boys approach. What Zitomer is to New York City, Robert's was to Cedarhurst. A little meet-and-greet capped off a fun-filled day in town.

Other times, I'd hit the big department stores with my mom. Yes, that's correct, plural. We'd hit at least three in a day. I remember waiting in line to be seated for lunch at the cafeteria inside, where we could finally put our shopping bags down and rest our weary feet. It was a sport after all, exhausting at times.

Shopping was so ingrained in the culture where I'm from that I recall an article published in our local paper, the Nassau Herald, about a classmate being allowed to buy one new piece of clothing each week. Imagine that display of consumerism even being newsworthy and making headlines. I recall reading with envy. I don't get to buy something once a week, I thought.

How it worked at my house was my mom would inspect my closet at the start of the school semester to assess the situation. Of course, I'd surreptitiously hide as much as I reasonably could in anticipation of this bi-annual visit. I always wondered how she didn't know. Lucky for me, her preoccupation with raising four kids on her own allowed me to get several more items to flaunt each season.

Where's my dad you might be wondering? I'm sad to

say, he lost a grueling battle with stomach cancer shortly after treating me to those hot pants. I never really felt I had enough time with him while he was alive. I was the youngest of four by a long shot, and my dad was always exhausted after a long day at work. So, we never had the chance to really bond. But, that's a story for another time.

As I look back at my young teenage years, I can distinguish them not only by what I was doing or the music I was listening to or who my friends and boy crushes were but by the clothes and shoes I was rocking. All the phases I went through...

Like when we all embroidered our well-worn jeans with colorful threads, mine depicted a smoking cig on the back pocket with the word PARTY. I felt so cool wearing them. I'm still sad I let those go.

Or the screen-print t-shirt trend. There was this happening place in the village on 7th Avenue near Christopher St. where we'd go to get them. We'd enthusiastically launch up the steep outdoor staircase to find all the latest screen print designs inside.

Back then, there were these vinyl-printed transfers that were applied with a high heat press onto the shrunken, fitted tees we wore. They had artworks of our favorite bands, like Led Zeppelin, and sayings of the moment like Right On or Keep on Truckin'. Or you could create your own sayings with felted letters. What a deeply satisfying experience it was getting custom t-shirts that reflected who we were and what we wanted to say. Everyone's dream is to be seen and heard. Well, at least mine. LOL.

Then, there was the denim overall trend that we wore with high-top construction boots in honey-colored leather or the time high-cuffed Levi's worn with Pro-keds was the Five Towns uniform.

One of my fave fashion moments was when belted three-quarter length coats with fur shawl collars had become de rigueur. Mine was in epic rust suede with beige shearling. Oh, so '70s.

There are too many to list really. But, one thing I can say with confidence is that we never ran around in workout clothing, thankfully. That was left for the gym.

Cut to 1974, the same year I wore out Bad Company's debut album. I remember running home to my mom and shouting out the big news...

> Me: I got a job!
> Mom: What do you mean? Where? Doing what?
> Me: The Esso station, pumping gas.
> Mom: What?! You're going to work at a gas station!?!
> Me: Yeah!
> (crickets...)
> Mom: Alright, we'll see how it goes.

I had just started smoking and used to buy my True Blue cigarettes there. After being encouraged by one of the cute young mechanics, I applied for a job. I was always boy crazy, so it didn't take much convincing.

Yeah, that was me in the midnight blue overalls with the dirty oil-stained rag sticking out of my back pocket pumping gas for all of a week or two. A couple more years and many fashion looks later, I would join the workforce again. But this time, it was something more closely aligned with my interests outside of boys.

Fashion Rising

At the age of sixteen, I landed my second job, this time on the retail selling floor at a boutique in town called Quasimodo. It was 1976, and Donna Summer's "Love to Love you Baby" and unisex designer denim were all the craze. It was also the year my secret crush, Steve Casiola, borrowed all my Donna Summer cassettes to copy and never returned them. Still stings. Not getting back the tapes, that is. But, I digress.

During this time, brands like Sasson and Gloria Vanderbilt ruled the fashion streets. And, of course, there was Calvin Klein with his risqué billboard ads that featured a fifteen year-old Brooke Shields seductively declaring, "Nothing comes between me and my Calvins." We wore our denim so tight back then, it was common to see people literally lie down on their backs to pull up their zippers. We'd instruct our customers that they were going to stretch so the tighter the better.

Quasimodo had this jeans bar, and yes, it was like a

bar. There was a counter, and all the denim was stacked behind in a wall of built-in wooden cubbies. We served the customer from there, first assessing and identifying what brands would look good on their frame, then pulling out a big stack and fingering through to find their size. Very high-touch customer service. Unbeknownst to me at the time, this job would set the trajectory for my 40-year career in fashion.

Acting and writing were my first loves, actually. Imagine a little kid wearing plaid bell bottoms, marching across an elevated brick fireplace hearth, belting out, "I'm going to Hollywood!" That was me. But, after dropping out of HB Studio, I knew I didn't have the dedication to the craft one needed to succeed, and waiting tables wasn't my jam. Besides, fashion came easily and naturally to me. Almost like I was born for it.

That same job exposed me to the world of retail buying. I was taken on a trip to the fashion trade shows in NYC, and my fashion star was born. That weekend, we went to the NAMSB show, the preeminent menswear venue back in the day, and the Boutique Show, which featured not only unisex fashions but a large section of bongs, pipes, rolling papers, incense, and candles.

It was the '70s. What can I say? Head shops were in abundance. Who'd have thought we'd kind of end up back there almost fifty years later, only legal this time? I chuckle.

It was a time when people had monikers like Crazy, Looney, Wedge, and Judge. I dated the latter three, and I especially remember Looney because he took me to the village one Saturday night, where he played his guitar on a Bleecker Street corner for tips. That part of Greenwich Village is where one of the last vestiges of an old New York still resides.

MacDougal Street, the part north of Houston, practically remains untouched in look and feel, all these decades later. I fondly remember scoring a cool psychedelic poster on MacDougal near Washington Square Park a few years earlier on one of our family jaunts into the city.

In 1977, the same year Fleetwood Mac debuted Rumours, one of my all-time favorite albums, my sister introduced me to her haircutting client, Timmy. A hottie, who knew how to dress, he was six years my senior and drove a brand-new Datsun 280Z in maroon. I remember the thrill of hearing his 5-speed engine shifting gears and getting louder as he got closer to my house. He introduced me to cocaine and the club scene emerging in New York.

The first club he took me to was called Infinity. No relation to Holly. This discotheque was at 683 Broadway, which was in a virtual ghost town back then. It had no name out front and no listing in the phone book. You only knew about it by word of mouth, as was the trend in those days.

It was thumping, a spot so exhilarating and massive that the restrooms were indicated by enormous neon signs, BOYS in blue and GIRLS in pink, so that you could see them from afar over the vast sea of dancing heads. There, you could do drugs in plain sight while sitting on stadium-sized bleachers or in rooms on the upper level, some crammed with mattresses. Oh, the decadence. Plato's Retreat, the infamous swingers club, opened that same year, as did the legendary discotheque, Studio 54.

The bridge and tunneler I was back then, we'd often double date with Timmy's cousin and his girlfriend du jour. We'd glide into Manhattan in his brand-new butter yellow Coupe de Ville to hit the dance floor. Songs like "Le Freak" by Chic and "Disco Inferno" by The Trammps got everyone moving. It was a time when dance crazes like the hustle and the bump ruled.

They were crazy times and only the beginning of my life in the famed New York scene that has fascinated Hollywood filmmakers and the world and would be depicted over and over again on the big screen.

Love, Loss and True Grit

ast forward, kicking off the decade of glitz, glam, self-indulgence and excess, it was 1980, and Blondie's single "Call Me" was number one. That year, I'd make the leap and leave my suburban town for a job in the big city. I remember telling my mom once again that I had gotten a job.

"Where?" she asked.

"The city!" I replied.

"The city...?" she said in an inquisitive tone.

"Yes, the city."

(crickets... again)

"Alright," she said apprehensively.

Ok, a little rewind here for context. I was tempted to just gloss over this, but I told you I'd leave it all on the stage. You see, up until this time, I had tried a bunch of things during high school and right after. All were short-lived and remain somewhat of a blur in my mind.

I was heavy into the party scene that was prevalent. Let's just say I experimented with everything except heroin. Ups, downs, angel dust, hash, weed, acid, the list goes on.

The entrepreneur in the making I was, even back then, I started my very first business dealing pot in between classes. We had this one side staircase into the building where everyone hung out and smoked. It was a time when narcs infiltrated the school system. It always struck me funny, and even to this day, that all they had to do was open that one set of doors to be hit with a huge cloud of stinky smoke and under it find kids getting high and me making deals to supply them.

Suffice to say, school took a backseat for a couple of years. My usual M.O. was to pick one course that I liked each semester and apply myself wholeheartedly, where I'd usually pull an A or B·. The rest fell by the wayside.

Finally, my teacher, Mr. Dibitetto, who incidentally was a hottie at 27 years old, and an organization called DECA got me back on track. By the time I was a senior, I actually won third place in a DECA statewide competition for a research project on emerging retail market trends. Not only was it a confidence boost at seventeen but a foreshadowing of my career to come.

Still, without enough credits to graduate with my class, I opted to take the GED versus repeating my senior year. No leaving me behind. I had lots to do with places to go and people to see. Plus, I couldn't bear the thought of another year at school without my friends by my side. Although I was still a bit unfocused, I explored and tried many different things — acting school, beauty school, and college, where I studied writing. But, none would have longevity, and dropout became the theme.

I later realized that a career in fashion was my destiny, because it was the one thing I circled back to that finally held my attention and I wanted to keep excelling at. Until that happened, though, with all my fits and starts and teenage drama, my mom was worn out, which brings us back to her apprehension over the news of my big leap to the big city for my shiny new job.

But, through it all, she was still my biggest cheerleader and willing to follow my lead. I imagine she was in awe of my fearlessness. She was sheltered to a degree and always applauded my drive and ambition. After all, she married a man 20 years her senior in an arranged marriage, had four kids and was a housewife up until the time my dad died.

I admired her more than I showed, though. Dressed in black for a full year of mourning, she took over running the family business after my dad passed. Day after day, she picked herself up, leaving the house at 6:30 am to open the grocery store my dad had built, literally, from the ground up. He constructed our family home and the building that housed what would be called Calamata Food Market at the same time.

This was the second move for the market into a space that was much bigger now, about half the size of a Trader Joe's. Its claim to fame was selling Greek and American products, produce and vegetables, and home-cooked Greek specialties like Spanakopita and Moussaka. I especially remember the imported feta cheese with its tart, robust flavor that arrived in sturdy wooden barrels.

When I wasn't helping my dad make change behind the counter that I could barely see over, I was eyeing the candy display. I'd get a small brown paper bag, like the ones some of his customers drank their beer out of, and fill it with candy bars like Mounds, Milky Way, Three Musketeers, and the latest, Nestle $100,000 bars. Oh, and M&Ms, another fave.

An immigrant, born in Cyprus, my dad came to America along with his brother, leaving behind their parents and seven other siblings. After being in the states for just a few years, he departed for the front lines to defend the United States in World War II. Well, the kitchen front lines. My dad had a cooking background, and in those days, they'd ask if you had any special abilities and assign you accordingly. He was an honest, loyal, and hardworking man who resolutely provided for us and made a damn good rice pudding.

My mom, whose parents emigrated from Greece, was born and raised in Scranton, PA. She was one of four kids and had survived her own war, suffering through great tragedy before meeting my dad. When she was a teenager, her twin sister was hit by a car and didn't survive. And just a handful of years before, another sibling was scalded in a kitchen accident and died at the age of three.

Independent of one another, my parents overcame a lot, and now after my dad's passing, it was time for my mom to step up as the sole provider. And she did so with courage and grit. After being held up at gunpoint one day, instead of closing up shop and rolling out of town quietly, my mom took shooting lessons and began toting a thirty-eight caliber. Mom didn't play.

She even went back to college and took up sculpting after selling the business and the building. At last tally, she had sixty-eight credits, which made her immensely proud. She was a badass in her own right. And I like to think I inherited some of my own badassery from her.

With my mom and dad as powers of example and the lessons I learned ingrained in my subconscious, it was now my time to venture out into the world, saying goodbye to Long Island...

Left: Daddy & me

Above: Channeling my inner YSL
with this peasant style dress

Below: Party time in my screen-printed
Yes band tee from the 7th Avenue shop,
circa 1972. Eye the poster of my fave band
at the time, Jethro Tull.

Getting my punk on

Hello, New York City!

Shortly after telling my mom I was going to work in the city, I dropped another bombshell. I was moving in with my boyfriend, Timmy. We got a place in Queens. Goodbye, Five Towns. See ya! I relished my newfound freedom living away from my mom for the first time and the fact that I was inching closer to Manhattan.

I'd drive my car to Forest Hills, park, and jump on the graffitied E train to the Citicorp 5th Avenue stop for my new job working as a sales associate at Bagatelle, a women's fashion retail store at 519 Madison Avenue. I remember feeling nervously excited as I navigated the midtown chaos to get there for my interview. But, they hired me on the spot and asked if I could start immediately. I must have wowed them with the hot pink cotton baggy pants and high heel nude mules I was wearing.

Located in the middle of high-rise office buildings, we'd be busy non-stop from 12-2 pm and again from 5-7 pm. This predictable daily rush felt like a stampede.

Imagine tons of suit-wearing women rushing on their lunch hour to get in and out. Think of the movie "Working Girl." They kind of looked like that. Hell, they were that. The movie was based on them!

Permed, big hair and shoulder pads, lots of shoulder pads. A little-known fact that always gets a look of disbelief is that shoulder pads weren't only in clothes but were also sold separately. The brands packaged them in canisters and were displayed by the check-out counter. The upsell item, they had these velcro loops that stuck to your bra straps. We'd wear them with everything - t-shirts, blouses, dresses, just to get that extra eighties lift.

Our visual merchandiser, Fred, who became a best friend, used to wear two pairs stacked under his oversized garment-dyed tees and long duster coat. All five-foot-four of him sauntering around with his full long locks grazing his inflated football shoulders. A sight to behold. LOL.

It was also around that time that NYC had its infamous mass transit strike when women chucked their pumps into totes in favor of wearing sneakers to commute. Imagine suit-clad women with their shoulder pads and big hair power-walking around in high-top Reeboks with scrunchy socks over their nylon pantyhose. You got it, funny as hell looking back. This gave such a feeling of comfort and emancipation traveling in their cushy trainers that the trend stuck around long after the strike ended.

Between the working girl rushes, the store looked like a tornado blew through. We'd have to go around and button, zip and properly hang the merchandise. We'd replenish the stock, check in boxes of new product, and hang and tag merch. We'd do these massive floor changes where we'd move all the inventory around and highlight previously hidden items and delight as they sold out. I always had a merchant mentality and loved to see things selling.

In those days, we had these big price ticket printing machines that we operated manually, registering the style number and color. After store rushes we'd sort the half tickets of the sold items and manually enter them one by one with pen on paper held in binders. We employed the old-fashioned tally mark method, four vertical lines and a crossed horizontal line made the fifth.

If memory serves, I was the one that came up with this early inventory management technique. Crazy old school, but it got the job done. It was new school at the time. LOL. No computers for years to come.

The store manager, who became a close friend, was named Chantal. She was a beautiful girl from Haiti who had a striking elegance and sophistication about her. She spoke French with the owners, Freddie and Albert, who were from Egypt. I learned a ton from them. With her gorgeous red lips and pulled back hair, Chantal turned me on to the drugstore, Duane Reade. With their big city selection, I was like a kid in a candy store. I had arrived.

Soon after I started at Bagatelle, my passion and hard work was recognized and rewarded when I was promoted to assistant manager and transferred to their location at 760 3rd Avenue. Life in New York City was looking up for this Long Island girl.

South Houston
Clothing Company,
circa 1981

The Downtown Retail Scene

n 1981, the same year disco dance track "Super Freak" by Rick James hit the scene, my bosses opened a new location at 20 West 8th Street called South Houston Clothing Company. Oddly, it was north of Houston Street, which New Yorkers express as HOW-stun, and pronounced like the city, Houston. But, I digress.

My bosses tapped me to be store manager. They also gave me a huge opportunity and bestowed upon me the esteemed title of Accessories Buyer. We carried mostly belts and handbags, plus socks and hosiery from brands like Hot Sox and Hue. Also EG Smith, those chunky, scrunched down socks worn with high top Reeboks by aerobics queens, oh, and those NYC commuters.

Thinking now, as I write this, they kind of got a twofer, manager and buyer. Two jobs, one salary. I was young and hungry and craved opportunity, and they knew it. I'd say it worked out for both of us.

At that time, 8th Street was the shopping equivalent of shoe heaven, with the most notable store being The

Village Cobbler located at one end. On the other end, just east of Fifth Avenue, sat the racy boutique, Patricia Field, that appealed to the club set and a whole host of celebrities and entertainers. Pat would later add costume design to her illustrious resume, co-creating the coveted looks in *Sex and the City* and the more recent *Emily in Paris*, with many notable projects in between, including *The Devil Wears Prada*.

With the street drawing an onslaught of shoppers daily, South Houston, which sold clothing and shoes, was poised for success. This was the hey-day of punk rock. And at the age of 20, with black-rimmed eye make-up, an asymmetrical haircut and stone-washed zip bottom Guess jeans, I ran that store like nobody's business.

The store was jamming since the day we opened the doors. We had to have a security person installed in the front to check in people's bags. During the madhouse, the line at the register was long, and my favorite times were when my assistant, David, and I manned the cash wrap to get people checked out fast, New York fast. We had a well-choreographed routine to ring up, process credit cards, de-security tag, fold, and bag the merch.

Theft was a big thing back then, and we caught many a shoplifter. They were prone to coming during the slow times when we were usually checking in boxes and organizing the store. We got to know the type. So, as soon as we spotted a suspicious person, down went the usually blasting music.

Someone would proceed to see if they needed help and nonchalantly follow them around a quiet store until they usually just left. Or there were the times we caught them red-handed, and they almost always responded in the same way, saying they didn't take anything as they peeled the new clothes off their bodies, which always struck me funny.

Even as members of the team, we were under a watchful eye. We were mandated to take periodic lie detector tests. I remember it was always so scary going down to the basement office, one by one, even though we had nothing to hide.

I also honed my skills in building a sale. When we'd get someone into a fitting room, we'd scour the store for more clothes and get some matching shoes, too. Wait, I'm feeling déjà vu.

I also spearheaded marketing initiatives. When stone washed denim was at its peak, my bestie, Fred, and I developed postcards to mail out. He did the graphic design and we wrote the copy together. We went back and forth and proofed the piece that was offset printed, the norm back then.

When we received the bulk postcard order we were mortified. You can imagine our surprise when the postcard adhered to the top of the brown carton said Let's get Stoned in Stone Washed Demins. We thought that line of copy was so clever. It became a running joke of ours. Just saying the word demin made us giggle.

The store always had its surprises like the time a lip curling, spiky-haired Billy Idol came in. And then, there was top model, Lauren Hutton, who bought two pairs of pointy-toed pumps by Caressa, one in taxi yellow and the other fire engine red. I checked her out at the register.

I later had the opportunity to go to her loft in NoHo

when I was a costume designer on an indie film. Since the film was low budget, we had to see what clothes she had that could work for her character. Excited to formally meet this icon, when the elevator doors opened into her loft, we were unexpectedly made to feel less than invited. That's show biz, I guess. Gotta be tough in this town and not take things too personally.

My bosses, capitalizing on the bounty of 8th Street, opened another store down the block from mine. By this time, all of the store managers from the other locations were my friends. A stone's throw from my store was One Fifth, the bar whose upstairs residents would later become the subjects of a book by Candace Bushnell, of *Sex and the City* fame. After a long day at work, we almost always ended up there. Our intention was a drink or two. But, three and five later, we'd still be there with lots to talk about!

Then, there were the days I got to leave the store and head into the accessory market to do my buying for the four stores we had by then. The accessories market stretched from the Empire State Building on 34th Street to around 40th Street, with showroom buildings dotted along 5th Avenue. The numbered side streets had more factories and trim houses between 5th and 6th Avenues mostly.

I remember Grandoe Accessories had this huge showroom with a full kitchen and a chef to feed the buyers. Satiated buyers write bigger orders, they say. LOL. Many brands were in the Empire State, too. With my fear of heights, I recall being nervous as the elevator careened up and down the floors of the 102-story skyscraper.

I remember Hot Sox bucked the norm and was at 1441 Broadway in the garment district. This may have been an omen for what would come next in my career. But, I won't spoil the story.

Pre-clubbing with Michele & Cathy

Sex in the City

ast forward to 1983. "Every Breath You Take" by The Police was number one, and after a drawn out breakup with Timmy, I moved into my first very own New York City apartment. It was a studio with super high ceilings at 154 West 70th St. Its claim to fame was that if you stuck your head out the window, to the left you could see Broadway. which I was only too excited to let everyone know.

It was a time when the sound of sirens and a sea of yellow taxis commandeered slick city streets and clouds of smoke emitted from pothole covers, when West 42nd Street was punctuated with hookers and dingy trench coat-clad men looking for peep shows. Yeah, that was New York in those days. Gritty, fast, and oh-so happening.

My store hours were 11-7. So, newly single with nowhere to be in the morning and New York as my playground, I was poised for good times and memories that would last a lifetime. Ahh, the glory days. Disco or punk, choose a camp. From Studio 54 to The Mudd Club and everything in between, clubbing was in full force.

This illustrious decade brought high-profile clubs that I'd frequent, such as the Tunnel, Palladium, Nell's, and The Limelight, which was housed in an old church and seemed radical at the time. Gothic in feel, it was built of stone and had ornate stained glass windows throughout. We'd party until the sun practically came up and then head to Lox Around the Clock to soak up all the alcohol in our bodies before bedtime.

Those were the days when a crescent shaped crowd would surround the club entrance. Self-proclaimed gods, the doormen hand-selected those they deemed worthy to enter. They would stand nonchalantly and look up every now and then and point. Usually, the best way to proceed was to sever the crowd with your body, striding confidently right up to the wine-colored velvet ropes like you belonged there.

Area was one of my favorites, with its revolving art installations. I can still remember the dopamine hit I felt when they opened the velvet rope to usher us up the steps and into the trendy downtown club. That hit stayed as we walked along the wide corridor with bass-thumping dance music getting louder with each step. The party was going on as much in the gender-neutral bathrooms as it was on the dance floor in those days.

These wild nights invariably ended up at the Empire Diner on 10th Avenue at around 4 am, where we'd eat a hearty bacon and egg breakfast. During this time, for reasons unknown to me now, I'd inevitably pick a fight with one of my friends. A verbal assault before heading home to sleep it off capped a great night. I can't say I was always an angel. But don't worry, we were all besties the next day and ready to do it all over again.

In between, I attended the Fashion Institute of Technology at night. My major was fashion buying and merchandising. In the cafeteria, I met Michele, who was from Brooklyn. She was a friendly, outgoing girl who was reeling from a recent breakup, which I would hear about for weeks.

She soon talked me into leaving my cherished studio with the Broadway view to get a place with her a couple of blocks over at 155 West 68th Street. I met Susan and Cathy through her, both beautiful and blonde and living together on the Upper East Side. Michele and I were the brunettes on the West Side to round out our foursome, the original *Sex and the City* crew.

I think of all the trials and tribulations we'd face as young twentysomethings navigating NYC in the '80s. Like Cathy's dilemma about whether she should fly to Hong Kong for the weekend to visit new love, Todd, who was there doing fashion production. Or what we should do when I lost the keys to Michele's boss's red corvette in the Hamptons. What was I thinking entering that club with no purse and the keys in my hand?

We'd do weekend brunches, then walk up and down Columbus Avenue to see and be seen. Restaurant bar scenes were of the moment. Friday nights, we'd do the West Side crawl. Columbus to Ruell's to Café Central, where a pre-fame Bruce Willis was bartender. These places were hopping three, four, five deep at the bar.

At Columbus, I remember feeling self-assured, and upon being introduced to rising Borscht Belt comedian

Jackie Mason, I promptly said, "Say something funny." He didn't. He kind of just stared at me, speechless for a minute.

It was a time of cavernous, noisy restaurants, with favorites like Ernie's and America leading the trend. It was also the early days of ultra-chic, iconic eateries, such as Indochine and The Odeon, and, of course, the beloved, legendary Serendipity, with its world-famous Frrrrozen hot chocolate dessert.

Further characterizing the decade, fitness centers, like the bougie Vertical Club on the East Side, started popping up, redefining the gym experience. And for those wishing to stay at home, Jane Fonda's aerobic workout tapes could keep you in shape. If that wasn't your jam, either, there was always rollerblading in Central Park while listening to your fave tunes on your Sony Walkman.

Charivari was the cutting-edge fashion retailer of the moment, whose famous ad campaign to snub the dawn of Banana Republic actually was prophetic to their fall. On public telephone booths, they had ads with khaki pants and white shirts and copy that read, "Wake us when it's over." Well, last I checked, Banana is still here and Charivari is not. Maybe they're still sleeping. Note to self: Evolve or die.

We'd vacation in the winter, going to Club Med, which had newly opened on a Caribbean island we'd never heard of before called Turquoise, short for Turks and Caicos. Before going to any hot spot in the winter, it was mandatory to hit the tanning beds to form our base coat so we wouldn't burn to a crisp when we got there. Slightly better than the metallic silver reflectors we used to sun ourselves in the seventies. Wink, wink.

We'd spend summer weekends in the Hamptons and dance the night away at Marakesh in Westhampton. On the ride out, we'd pass the town of Shinnecock, purposely mispronouncing its sign as we sped by. In our best British accents we'd say, "Shine Cock, where the men stand off to the side of the road and shine their cocks." I can't believe I'm telling this story. LOL.

I vividly remember coming back from one such weekend and hitting Columbus for a late Sunday afternoon stroll when I ran into my boyfriend, Simon (pronounced see-MAW), with his arm wrapped around an unknown woman. I guess it's true what they say about French men. Very charismatic, they can make you feel like you're the only one on the planet. More about the French invasion later.

Then, there was the time that Cathy was dating this guy who managed the leather boutique on Bleecker Street. A hot model type, he had a sweeping, dirty-blonde mane of hair. Think cover of a romance novel. That look. Once holding promise, things went south after he physically roughed her up one night.

We had several ensuing conversations on how we collectively should handle this. Well, she left him and, in case you were wondering, yes, she did meet Todd in Hong Kong for the weekend. Crazy adventurers we were.

For New Year's one year, we went skiing in Vermont. We drove up in a blizzard at night. Michele or "Charles in Charge," as we affectionately called her by then, was driving, and we had to navigate treacherous, windy roads up the mountain.

Venturing out the next day on a clear, sunny morning, we were shocked to see the steep drop-offs. Our thoughts raced to how we could have slid off the mountain in our rental. The weekend hit a high point when we did ecstasy. It was my first time, and we were all lovey dovey on the small dance floor in the wood-paneled lodge.

We navigated through all of the fashion trends together as a foursome, too. We each had our individual style. Whether wearing duster coats, harem pants, tunic tops and lycra stirrups, or banana clips in our hair, we rocked it our own way.

Around this time, Michelle, Fred and I discovered Montreal. It was the first of several trips we would take together. Sometimes our Londoner friends, who were also in fashion, would come along, too.

Take-off to touch-down was 50 minutes, and we were in the closest thing to Europe you could get without going there. The dollar was super strong, and we'd shop Saint Catherine Street like celebrities, going in and out of stores, like "it" retailer Mousseline, with the sales staff fawning over us. Rich New Yorkers, they thought, I'm sure. Being a New York native has always been met with a sense of awe wherever I've traveled.

We stayed at the Four Seasons, along with the real celebrities like Madonna, when she was on her Blonde Ambition tour. I distinctly remember being seated in the lobby when she was swiftly escorted through to the elevator-in-waiting in a beige menswear suit with her short, bleach blonde haircut, a chic new look for the black lace-wearing pop star. We also saw U2 while staying there during their Zoo TV tour. It was all so exciting and such an ego bump. Oh, and I met Richard on our first trip there. More on him later.

Above: Shopping trio, Michele, Fred and me, on one of our jaunts to Montreal

Below: Fred and I cracking up over the word "demin" probably. Note the extreme shoulder pads.

Right: The original *Sex and the City* crew, Michele, Susan, Cathy, and moi, circa 1983

Iconic New York City subway.
"You talkin' to me?"

The Uptown Days
& the Big Pivot

One day, my friend, and one-time girlfriend to my brother, Vivian, who was the clothing buyer at South Houston, left and tapped me to join her at Orva, a brand new 7,500 square foot store at 155 East 86th St. Coming from 1,500 square feet, that was a big step up. With department managers under me, I would be the big kahuna, general manager, overseeing it all.

Bigger title, more responsibility and more money, lots more money. I was in. The only problem was I would no longer be buying. No trips to the showrooms. No cool downtown vibe. No happy hours at One Fifth. And I was no longer left to manage a store without oversight.

After seven excruciating months in a slow-moving store and the five-foot-three suit-clad owner pacing around, seemingly breathing down my neck, scrutinizing my every move, I was done. You can't pay me enough, I thought. I learned then that if what you're doing is killing your joy, it's best to cut your losses and

41

move on, or up as it was in my case.

A couple of phone calls later, I got a job as an accessories buyer for the 34th Street Bootery. A busy store down the block from the world's largest store, Macy's. The twenty-five percent pay cut didn't matter to me, because I was back on the right career path in an exciting, promising, new environment.

Buying fed my soul creatively, and that was the most important thing to me, oh, and being in a place that was hot and happening. West 34th Street was definitely that. Teeming with pedestrian traffic, one had to employ the New York bob and weave technique to get past people.

When I wasn't in my office in the back of this pumping store, I got to go into the market and buy everything from Madonna-inspired lace fingerless gloves to glam rhinestone jewelry, from belts and bags to scarves. It was then that I had a fashion revelation while speaking to my sales rep. We agreed that animal prints defied the trends and are always in style with the people who love them. Still holds true today.

Nothing energized me more than seeing the things I bought flying out. I loved being the reorder queen on Mondays.

It was here that I was exposed to the shoe industry in a whole new way. My boss, Albert, took me to trade shows in hotels, where we sat on carpeted floors examining and dissecting shoes. I learned about lasts, vamps, and shafts and how to build new styles.

It was creative and fun having the power to customize them for our stores and put our own label inside. An early case of private label experience. Months later, these creations would arrive at our stores from places like Brazil, Spain, and Italy. No one would have dreamed then that China would ever make shoes. It was an absurd thought. Plastic maybe, but leather? No way.

Vintage band jacket ala Michael
Jackson. I felt like hot shit wearing that
outfit to the clubs.

Honing My Craft

Cut to 1985. New wave music was going viral. Tears for Fears released their anthem, "Shout." And I was promoted to clothing buyer for the Bootery's other store named Topaz, coincidentally my birthstone, where I'd work under Albert's brother, Soly.

I sat right outside his office, and we went around the garment district daily like Batman & Robin, conquering fashion's pressing dilemmas. The wall clock would hit 12 pm, and we were off. We'd walk a few blocks to the garment center, and Soly would treat me to lunch, where we frequently ran into his friends with their buyers.

One of our usual spots was Jerusalem, a boisterous cafeteria-style eatery that offered Middle Eastern fare and was usually packed by the time we got there. We'd slowly push our platters along the metal railing, choosing things like falafel, Israeli salad and hummus platters.

If we were feeling fancy, we'd go to Mr. Broadway, a kosher deli. Pastrami on rye with pickles on the side for

45

me. And then, there was always the coffee shop in the lobby of 1407 Broadway, which, back then, was one of the hottest showroom buildings and where it wasn't unusual to find sales reps exiting their offices with white powder on their noses.

After a quick bite, we'd start our fashion hunt. In those days, the garment district consisted of skyscraper showroom buildings on Broadway and 7th Avenue, aka Fashion Avenue. Each building was dedicated to specific markets, such as swimwear, coats, designer, bridal, couture, dresses, kids, juniors, contemporary, missy, bridge, etc. The rest of the trade took place on the numbered side streets and along 8th Avenue, where you'd find factories, warehouses, pattern rooms, trim houses, jobbers, printers, and fabric stores.

It was popping everywhere. Strong men navigated rolling racks with finished goods on hangers in poly bags swishing through the bustling city streets. There were factory workers pushing sturdy rectangular canvas hampers with cut work inside. UPS drivers plowed through with boxes piled so high you couldn't see their faces.

We visited everything from glossy showrooms to stodgy factory-warehouses, where we'd often work directly with the brand owners. I learned so much from Soly about buying and negotiation, how to extract the key items from a collection and get them for the best price. Spot the item, exploit the item, rinse and repeat.

We had a big pencil, as we'd say back then, which was the ability to write some nice, chunky orders. Having five retail doors that did high volume meant we had leverage when we asked for a discount. No order got placed without it.

He also showed me the ways of fobbing. This has no correlation with the definition in the dictionary. Don't bother looking it up. Fobbing is buying the brands that have high recognition and are usually higher priced due to their branding, but then going into the market and buying lesser known brands or even creating your own private label programs that sell for less with significantly higher margins.

Back then, the branded merchandise usually had at least a keystone markup, meaning double the price we paid or more, while our programs garnered three and four times markup. The well-known brands made the store look good and positioned it higher, while the lower-priced merch appeared to be of higher value, and customers would dig in and buy more. That merch is where the real money is made, and we were able to go through hundreds of pieces of a style in a busy weekend.

It was an opportune start for me to learn about the product development process. Soly was a partner in a brand called JouJou that was hot at the time and designed these massive collections. I was first introduced to them when I started at Bagatelle. We sold their spandex disco pants that came in a rainbow of bright colors. Think Olivia Newton John in Grease. That style put them on the map. All it takes is one hot item to make a beginning in fashion. True then and still is today.

We'd convene at the JouJou offices at 525 7th Avenue and put our programs together in the big conference room. The meetings usually started with us knocking off our bestselling styles and adding some others to round out the assortment. We once did this huge program of CP Shades-looking, oversized, yummy, garment dyed separates in an array of colors. Blew out and reordered multiple times.

At Topaz, I learned another valuable lesson that's about timing the market. After an item is blowing out and reordering, beware of the final reorder that just sits. You don't know when it will happen. But, it usually does, if you're not careful. I had to keep a close eye out for this sometimes subtle turn.

Imagine a swinging trapeze. When you can grab it at the very start, it takes you for a long ride. Fashion is like that. If you adopt a trend in its infancy you can milk it the longest. If you get on in the middle, when it's starting to get saturated, you have less time and more competition. And if you were sleeping and try to jump on at the end, well, it's the end. Whatever goes up must come down.

If you're lucky, sales begin to slow, and you begin to see the market getting inundated with the same style, giving you a heads-up. In other cases, it just drops dead one day. Boom, just like that. Sometimes, it's best to adopt an attitude of "Quit while you're ahead." and move on to the next trend.

I was always on the lookout for the next big fashion wave. As it is in life, timing is everything in fashion. Being too early is just as bad as being too late. Sometimes, you have the foresight to try something, and it doesn't retail. Then, a year later, it's the hottest thing, and you're gun-shy to buy in again.

This is where gut and intuition play into the equation. Everyone is so data-focused these days, which is super useful and has its place. But instinct? That can't be processed by a computer.

It was also during this time that I learned a lot more about color's impact on fashion. I saw how women gravitated toward certain shades based on their complexion and ethnicity. Shifting color trends also ruled the seasons, like when fuchsia and cobalt blue were everywhere or the season everything we bought in olive drab sold out, or as we routinely called it, O.D.

We also went through a phase when we bought vintage items from Antique Boutique, which had a store on lower Broadway near NYU. We'd pick a silhouette, and they'd come assorted naturally, since they were all one of a kind. I recall the time we were blowing out of men's tweed overcoats. Think of Brat Packer Judd Nelson in The Breakfast Club. Girls were wearing them, too, oversized. That was the look.

It was at Topaz that I went on my first of many buying trips to Los Angeles to shop the showrooms at the original Calmart, which consisted of only three building towers labeled A, B, and C. I remember going into a showroom where I was introduced to an unknown designer who made these white tees printed with black stick figures. While it was not right for my stores then, you may know the casual lifestyle brand Michael Starrs all these years later. It was exciting to see the brands evolve and develop over time.

The Calmart was miniature in comparison to the whole of the NYC garment center. Therefore, it was much easier to shop as a buyer. With only three buildings that were interconnected, it was a breeze walking through the corridors where the showrooms had floor to ceiling glass windows that we could peer into. The types of fashion were further segmented by building letter and floor number.

After shopping the showrooms downtown, we'd hit the retail stores to find interesting labels we didn't know so we could locate them in the market the following day. In those days, a lot of the fashion trends started in LA before migrating to the East Coast. We wanted to be there to capitalize on being first to market with the newest trends emerging.

At night, we went to trendy restaurants on the Sunset Strip, such as Nicky Blair's and Spago. We'd spot A-list celebrities there, and it was the first time I would see a band of paparazzi loitering out front waiting for that bespoke shot they could sell to the tabloids. LA was popping and fast became my home away from home.

We also went to Montreal to shop in their garment district on Chabanel Street, the most notable building being 555. Another big break came when I was brought along to shop for our stores in the Parisian fashion district in the Sentier, and my lifelong love affair began with the city of lights. We'd walk down narrow streets lined with storefronts housing tons of merchandise on racks.

It was there that Soly introduced me to one such shop that he deemed to have the best merch. They distributed a variety of brands. I met the owner, a chic Parisian woman named Colette who exhibited strength in her demeanor. Sound familiar to some of you? Yes, she went on to open the famed fashion concept store of the same name on Rue Saint-Honoré that every global fashionista paid pilgrimage to while in Paris. Well, I can say I knew her when.

Next, I graduated to a solo London trip, and I remember feeling fancy staying at the Hilton on Hyde Park. London was and is super cool. Though, I can't help but recall the astonishment I felt when I unexpectedly drove by Buckingham Palace, and there it was, right off the busy road. No mysterious, long driveway like I'd imagined. There it stood, naked with gates and guards, practically on a traffic circle.

The name of the game always was as follows: How can we be trend forward and different by having the merch no one else has or choosing and merchandising the brands in a way no one else would? How can we stand out with our unique point of view, aka POV? Unbeknownst to me at the time, I was being conditioned to always be innovating and on the hunt for the extraordinary.

I met a lot of people along the way and my buying efforts did not go unnoticed. I was once approached by a Canadian fashion entrepreneur named Brian, who offered to potentially back me financially in a store of my own. Giddy at the notion, when he asked for a business plan, I fastidiously assembled a plan for what the store build-out would look like and all the incredible brands I would carry. If you know anything about business plans, they don't look like that. I came to realize what a naïve attempt that was. Live and learn. LOL.

Early eighties style. Feeling cutesy.

The French Invasion

During my tenure at Topaz, we witnessed what I'll call the French invasion of the garment district on West 37th Street. Others called them Euro-trash, a derogatory term reserved for stylish and affluent European expats. All the Parisian garmentos, including cheater Simon, bringing the coolest brands, set up shop there to distribute their wares to retailers, many on a cash-and-carry basis. Storefronts lined the street like I had seen in Paris, with brands like Naf Naf and Petit Bateau.

When you walked in, it wasn't unusual to see the styles hanging on display and brown open cartons on the floor with flat packed garments overflowing or poly-bagged merchandise hung on pipe racks. That was the inventory they had on hand, so you would pay first and either take it with you or have them ship it immediately. At Topaz, on the other hand, we never paid upfront, since we always negotiated credit terms.

Somewhat similar operations existed throughout the garment district and were known as jobbers. Though, for the most part, that merchandise was not branded or contemporary and was usually sold to stores out of the country like South America. West 37th Street was different. The Europeans added a chic flair to our garment center.

Soly and my old boss from Bagatelle, Freddie, who were besties, got in on the street action when they joint ventured in a partnership to import and distribute the London brand Pamplemousse. They decked out the space in Memphis style décor, which was newly trending at the time. Think primary colors and geometric shapes.

I connected my roommate, Michele, and she got a job running the place. I'd pretty much stop there on the daily to check-in between my showroom appointments. From the conference room, we'd coordinate our Montreal trips and other plans, like making our Thursday night dinner rezos. No real New Yorker ever went out on the weekends since the city was flooded with bridge and tunnelers. Ahhh, how far I'd come.

In those days, everything was so schmoozy, and nothing ever really felt like work. Being paid to bounce around, shop, travel, explore my creativity, see new and exciting fashion, meet and hang out with old friends and new people... What could be wrong with that? Gotta love the good old days!

Bye Bye, New York
Hello, Montreal!

ventually, the day came when I left Topaz for no other reason than to move to Montreal with my soon-to-be Canadian husband, Richard, who I met on that first trip to Montreal while he was slinging shoes at Joan & David, a hot footwear brand at the time. It was 1987, the year U2 released The Joshua Tree and we'd see them in concert three times.

Over the course of a long distance romance, we fell in love, and Richard moved to New York to live with me for a year or so. But, without a visa to work, he struggled to find a good-paying job, which really put a strain on us. So, we made the decision to try Montreal for a while.

With the cost of living so low there, we moved into a luxury high-rise in downtown Montreal on Peel Street just north of Sherbrooke. From our balcony, we could see the cityscape, and all was great until we were awakened on our first morning by jackhammers. Not sure how we missed that construction was happening on the adjacent plot of land when snagging the place.

Obliviously in love we were. What can I say?

I landed a job seemingly overnight as a buying consultant for a 32-store chain based there named Mia. New York carried clout, I learned. They even leased me a car. I had to drive out of my chic downtown locale to the desolate industrial area with low building complexes that suggested manufacturing, warehousing and other non-glamourous activities.

We were so remote a food truck, or as we called it in New York, a roach coach, would come in the morning and at lunchtime. Once you got there, you weren't leaving. Plus, with the sub-zero temperatures, who wanted to go out anyway, lest their nose hairs froze? No kidding, it actually happened to me. It's true what they say about Canadian winters.

Back inside were offices, of which I had my own, and a big conference room. And then, there was my boss's office, whose last name escapes me, though we referred to him formally as Mister. This was all attached to a huge warehouse where we received every shipment for the thirty-two stores in the chain.

Monday mornings, the rest of the buying team and I arrived to find a huge selling report on our desks. It consisted of white and light green striped landscape pages that were held together by perforations and fed through a dot matrix printer. This was a loud, squeaky machine with a mechanism that traveled back and forth horizontally on each page, emitting ink, and as the paper passed through, there was a wire basket below to collect the clunky report. All in all, it was a vast improvement from the manual tally system I first employed at Bagatelle.

Always fascinated to see how we did after the busy weekend, I'd eagerly peruse the report and circle the items with the best sell-thrus. I also identified slow moving ones. Anything in between was just that, middle of the road; not much to do there, yet.

We'd assemble as a team afterward and share our insights and determine any next steps we'd take. These could be reordering styles and/or marking down the slowest sellers based on when they were received. The most important thing we gleaned was whether or not we were seeing an emergence of a trend.

If yes, we went out into the market like moths to a glittering flame to find ways to exploit it. We had a directive, and we were on a mission of epic proportion. This is where the real money is made. You'll invariably do 80% of your business on 20% of the styles, so it goes. That's why it's mission critical to spot any emerging trend.

On an average day, we'd head into the market and hit the showrooms and take notes on the styles we liked best. After that, an assistant would contact all the sales reps to tell them we were having a style-out. One by one, our requests would be dropped off at our industrial complex. We'd then have a big meeting with the merch scattered about our conference room. We'd switch back and forth with some of us standing and others seated as we touched, inspected and tried on the clothes.

Things were chosen while others were discarded. Often, more than one brand had similar looks, and sometimes, we'd have to debate to agree on a winner. We'd determine where the holes were categorically in the assortment and create a hit list of what still needed to be found. The hunt is never over as a buyer.

The meetings went on for hours. By the end, we were exhausted. But, our job was done for the day. We managed to pull together an assortment that women would be wearing on the street in the coming weeks and months.

Sometimes, after these meetings, I'd be called into Mister's office, which seemed dimly lit by my recollection now. But, I think that's because the rest of the place was all decked out in fluorescent lights. I'd sit across from him, looking over his huge wooden desk, and he'd ask me, in a serious tone, how things were going. I get the sense now that, because I was from New York, he thought I had magical, mysterious insights to impart from the big city, like a spirit guide.

As much as I enjoyed my role at Mia and the respect Mister bestowed upon me, at age 27, Montreal felt like a sleepy town compared to where I came from. It's difficult to find a place that can hold a candle to New York City. Call me biased, but it's true, at least to me.

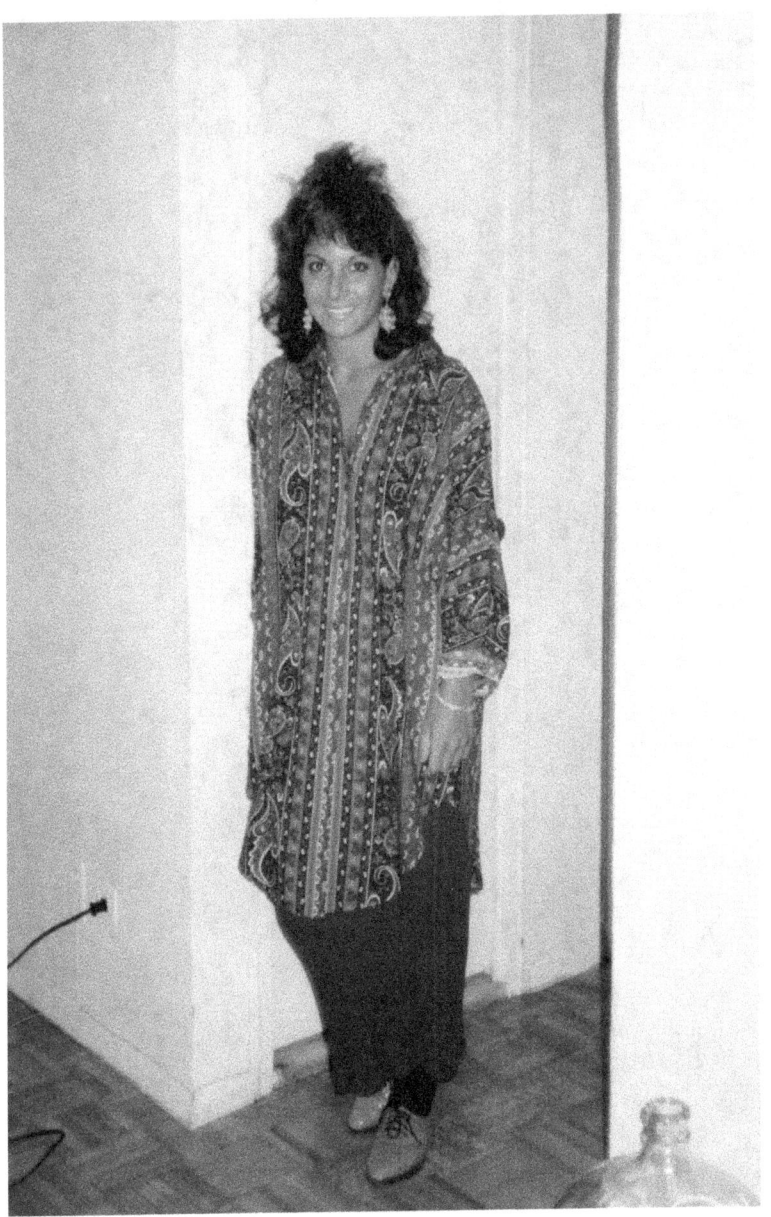

Feeling Boy George vibes for some reason

Richard & me when we had just moved to Montreal. Yes, that's a cardboard box we are eating on and lawn furniture we are sitting on. LOL.

On my first buying
trip to LA. Acid wash
was all the rage.

Hello & Goodbye Times Two is Born

ith New York calling me home, when one of my suppliers, a Montreal-based vertical knitwear mill, approached me to help them open a showroom there, I couldn't say yes fast enough. Timing is everything in life. I intuitively knew this period in NYC would be culturally unprecedented and couldn't bear to miss another minute (early case of FOMO). Turns out, it was a dry run of what I would create for myself later.

I landed us a fine space at 209 West 38th Street. I felt important, having been given the responsibility of finding the showroom and setting it all up with its furnishings. Working on my own, I got busy calling buyers and had moderate success getting them in to see this new collection. Though, one by one, they declined when they found out the sweaters were made of acrylic.

Even though they were well-designed in beautiful colors, with high-end weaving and finishing techniques, they were still acrylic. That yarn just had a bad connotation that equated it with something cheap. Had these same styles been cotton, the buyers would have been interested. But, the mill wasn't amenable to making any changes. And after roughly six months of rejections, I was out and so were they from the US market.

I was relieved to go back to a New York City buying gig for the next year or so after the acrylic fiasco. In hindsight, I probably should have known acrylic could be a dealbreaker. But, in my defense, the styling and quality were so good, and it was retailing really well for me in Canada. Another valuable lesson learned: Regional markets have their preferences.

Cut to 1989, a year that will never be forgotten, and not because of the music. My brother, Chris, succumbed to his three-year battle with HIV, my mom was suddenly diagnosed with stage 4 lung cancer, and I decided to start my first business.

They died less than six weeks apart. I know my mom hid her illness and secretly didn't want to witness her firstborn dying. Chris died first, but my mom never knew because the cancer had metastasized to her brain, so she was rarely coherent in the end. It was rough going into Long Island Jewish Hospital and traversing between floors to visit them both.

I don't wish what I went through on anyone. It was an extraordinarily painful time that I dealt with by putting blinders on and just forging ahead like it never happened. Don't feel, just move. Make no mistake, though. In private, I had hysterical bouts routinely, and I would be forever changed.

While realizing how short and fragile life was, I was growing more dissatisfied with working for the man.

Well, actually, there were two, and they were brothers. They owned the stores I was buying for. One was the kindest man, and the other a ruthless you know what. A real Dr. Jekyll and Mr. Hyde situation. When I asked for a pay raise, the ruthless one became incensed at the notion that I would have the gall to even think they weren't paying me enough money.

Looking back, I was being bullied but didn't have the language for it. But, I knew I was being condescended to and that he was treating me unfairly. So, I did the only right and respectable thing and made the executive decision to quit... on the spot. Boom, take that!

I always had the dream of having my own store. But, covering the cost of getting a lease, building it out, and stocking it with merchandise was, well, just that, a dream. I had no savings and pretty much lived paycheck to paycheck. So, when I made that declaration and marched out of the office that day what was I going to do?

It was time to make my move. I clearly remember my boss Soly telling me on more than one occasion that I needed to work for myself. I was an independent thinker with so many ideas and a strong personality. I wanted things done my way. So, with a little bit of thought, I recognized there was an opportunity that stood before me.

The brands I was buying from either had their own showroom, known as a corporate showroom, or they were represented by showrooms that housed up to several brands. These were known as independent sales reps. I suddenly thought of a girl named Candy. She worked in one of those so-called corporate showrooms when I first met her. But, recently, I had seen her somewhere else.

She was by herself, and a variety of collections lined the walls in her tiny new space. Could she have made the leap to open her own showroom? She didn't seem that sharp to me. Hmm... I figured that if Candy could do it, I could definitely do it.

I was ready to stuff all that grief and just carry on like it never happened. So, with fierce grit and determination, plus a $1500 credit card cash advance, I threw myself into my exciting, new business. After all, what could be better than being a fashion entrepreneur in New York City? The ruler of my own domain, calling all the shots. Do what I want, when I want.

Blinders on, I forged ahead like a freight train in the night, kicking ass and taking names. Times Two Sales Agency was born.

Thirteen years of experience in the industry taught me a ton about the dos and don'ts of business. My bosses, who I worked closely with, had bootstrapped their companies. These were hard-working entrepreneurs who had real success with bottom lines to match and were crushing it in a tough town. They were my mentors. I knew if I could employ even a fraction of what I had learned, I'd soon be crushing it, too!

At that time, the heart of the NYC garment district spanned W 35th St. to W 42nd St. from Broadway to 8th Avenue. After shopping in the showroom buildings for years, I knew that being in the right one was imperative. While buyers may have needed to go to other buildings, 1466 Broadway was home to the majority of brands in the advanced contemporary market.

These buyers came to 1466 frequently and stayed all day. In those days, they could discern what you were about based on which building you were in. So, armed with the knowledge that this was the place to be, I was effectively positioning my showroom.

In the very beginning, Richard, who was my husband by then, was my wingman. We worked together in those early months of the company. As fate would have it, the Pret-A-Porter trade show was happening within days of my sudden revolt against the brothers. (They purposely remain nameless, though I did like the nice one.)

We attended the show so I could scope out lines that didn't have sales representation in New York. Brands were sold primarily through wholesale channels back then. Making intros and networking, handing out business cards, we began.

I remembered a brand out of Philly that I sold really well when I was a buyer. They didn't have a showroom in New York, so I reached out. Richard and I drove to Philly to make the deal. The owner was Vietnamese and took us for dim sum. We were ecstatic being wined and dined, as was the norm in those days.

There, we wowed him with how much more business he would do by having a sales rep in NYC that would be selling his brand 24/7. He agreed, and just like that, we signed our first brand, or so we thought. Excited, we returned to the city, where I had already laid the groundwork to make a deal with someone who had a showroom in 1466.

Panos was that someone. He was from Greece, and I knew him because he had tried selling to me. I also knew he didn't have his shit together because he frequently didn't have his samples. When asked about when they would arrive, his canned response was always, "Fifteen days." So, I befriended him and approached him with the idea that I rent part of his showroom, and he agreed.

It was a great location, right off the elevator. We would occupy a small fraction of his shoebox-sized showroom for $900 a month. We had a verbal agreement in place and were ready to go. Amazing!

But then, our Philly brand contacted us. He was pulling back and didn't want to make the deal. Offering no solid reason beyond that, I figured he likely didn't want to pay our 10% commission. He never got a showroom and eventually seemed to fade away. Sometimes, you have to start before you're entirely ready.

The Defining Moment

So, I had no brand to start and a showroom that cost $900 a month. Deflated, I sought the advice of one of my trusted sales rep friends who I used to buy from. Steve was from Parasuco, a denim brand out of Montreal. Think acid washed denim from the '80s. I think they started the trend in fact.

Steve told me in no uncertain terms. "Take the showroom. You'll get a line." I remember it like it was yesterday. That was my "Build it, and they will come." moment. The synchronicity of it all is not lost on me, looking back. It could have easily gone either way that day.

Steve's encouragement and seeming trust in my potential propelled me forward. The belief in your endeavor from someone you respect is powerful. So, with that and a fierce determination, I took the showroom. And the brands and buyers came, and I never looked back.

None of this would have happened if I didn't effectively build it first. I had to have the groundwork laid out. I think it was the energetic intention I was setting by taking the showroom, plus lots of hard work and a sprinkling of luck.

Today, that phrase is met with criticism mostly. People say building it won't make them come. I think what they're referring to is the fact that you can't just build it and wait for something to magically happen.

On the contrary, I got out there and leveraged every connection I had built to that point. My mission was two-fold. Find new brands to represent and sell to the buyers, and find buyers that would buy the brands. And so I did.

Although I was opening my sales and marketing agency with little sales rep experience (Remember the acrylic fiasco?), I had two things going for me. I had sat on the other side of the buying table for years, witnessing my sales reps, and I had a good eye for buying. I was able to effortlessly translate my skill of trendspotting into finding good, slash that, great saleable lines to represent. And armed with the notion that if Candy could do it so could I, I forged ahead.

No Way but Up

The fourth floor at 1466 felt less like a building where business was transacted and more like a college dorm. Occupants would drop in on one another just to chat. It was one big water cooler party. There were characters like long-haired Jack from Hard Tail with a cig always hanging from his mouth (RIP Jack.) or the cute boys that worked at Tripp NYC and Stussy.

We'd talk about everything from our plans for the weekend to what new stores had opened, which ones had credit and which ones weren't paying their bills. If we had heard of a store and what our experience was. Which ones bounced shipments and checks and which ones always wanted an RTV, that's a return-to-vendor. Was someone going out of business? Were they filing chapter 11? We all helped each other in those ways. I felt like we could have been part of a sitcom. Think *Cheers*, only, instead of a bar, the fourth floor was our soundstage.

Richard and I made our first hire, a part-time assistant who came to New York to fulfill her dreams of becoming a dancer. With the strict discipline and grace of a ballerina, Paige was punctual, efficient, and had great penmanship, which was a bonus since it was BC, before computers. She did data-entry, bookkeeping and any other things we needed done for our fledgling enterprise.

Several weeks in, Richard resumed working on the outside to bring in more money so we could continue to organically grow the business. We intentionally kept our expenses low by moving to Hell's Kitchen. The area was still pretty grunge and desolate on 11th Avenue. So, we scored a great deal on a one-bedroom in a luxury doorman building, with a balcony and a view of the Empire State.

Our big splurge would be going to La Marca on Third Ave and 22nd Street, where they made amazing home-cooked Italian food. It was a small place, cafeteria style. We would bring a bottle of red and, for thirty bucks, we felt like royalty.

My first big break would come a couple months into my repping. By this time, I had managed to get a few lines, mostly people I met at the Pret Show. The business was being floated with those early brands, who paid a $500 showroom fee and a $1000 draw against commission monthly. There was no doubt in my mind that we were on the right track, focusing on the future, never looking back.

The Making of a Trend

One day, I got a call from Alan, a rep I was friendly with from my buying days. He had a line he couldn't keep because it conflicted with another collection he had and asked if I wanted to see it. So, I headed over to his showroom.

He opened the closet door and there it was: an unimpressive, broken-down cardboard box on the floor. He dragged it out, and I peeked in to see crumpled rayon separates carelessly thrown in, mostly in burnt orange with some coconut beaded fringe trim, nothing show-stopping. But, I knew this fabric was retailing on the conflicting line, and all I was thinking was, I'll take the box and talk to the owner. Nothing ventured, nothing gained.

A man in his fifties, the owner Denny, was in Los Angeles and exuded lots of high energy in our interactions. Based on our initial discussion, we clicked, and I felt like he was keen to understand why this industry veteran should give his line to a much younger newbie. Mind you, he was keeping the lights on in his factory making scrunchies.

And I don't think any reps were falling over themselves to take his copycat line. So, I think we both needed our break. The more we spoke, the more rapport we built, and his brand, Average Joe, was signed to the showroom. But wait, there's more to the story.

A couple of weeks into having the line, he tells me changes are coming. A rep in LA by the name of Lourdes, who had her finger on the pulse of things, started directing the company to a full rebrand. New fabric, new look, new name, Mica was born and so was the floral printed California dress trend that typified much of the coming decade.

The baby doll trend followed behind with their crochet lace tiered number. We got busy launching this brand, and it was like candy to a kid. My showroom went from the new and obscure to the new and hot one to watch practically overnight.

I started regular trips to LA, where I'd stay at Denny and his wife, Judy's, Hollywood Hills house, right above Sunset and La Cienega. Judy was no bullshit and a driving force in the operations of the company. Denny and I would hit the downtown factory, and I learned all about the business from the manufacturing side.

I was brought into the line development process and helped pick out rayon prints we'd source from India. Later, we started developing our own. One such print was inspired by these small antique perfume bottles that caught my eye while I was taking a steam bath in their master suite. It was a hit. I realized then I had a knack for prints, a skill I would hone and amplify throughout my career.

We'd shop the stores and meet with the owners and get the 411 on what they were selling. We'd meet with Lourdes in her showroom. The mean girl she was, I sensed her fierce competitiveness and desire to be number one. With me driving sales on the East Coast and her on the West, we didn't get too tangled.

There'd be no love lost when Denny eventually tired of her narcissistic ways and replaced her with Michele, who oversaw sales as the company grew and grew. She and I would come to share many valuable business insights and glasses of Chardonnay over time. Though my hard partying days were behind me, wine could still save the day.

At night, Denny would run me around LA, taking me to legendary old Hollywood places like Musso & Frank's. On the weekends, he'd take me to Duke's on Sunset for pancakes. I got the sense Denny relished the rich history of his town and proudly wanted to share it. He'd implore me to jump on the back of his Harley even though I was afraid of bikes. Or we'd tool around in his pride and joy, a classic red Thunderbird convertible.

He surprised me with tickets to Arsenio one time, who was the trending late-night talk show host. Another time, he got me in to see a tribute to Dick Clark of American Bandstand, where I sat across from 70's heartthrob David Cassidy from the Partridge Family. With his buzzed haircut and Barbie-pink suit, he didn't seem nearly as cool as I remembered, decked out in his brown suede fringe jacket and shag haircut all those years ago. But, I digress.

The stellar moment happened when Denny took me to the 63rd Academy Awards, a night I'll never forget. Not just because it was such a surreal opportunity and I walked the red carpet but also because somewhere midway through the evening, in a blur, Denny got up, gestured to me and whisked me down an orchestra aisle where all the celebs were seated and ushered me toward two vacant seats at the end.

I was still settling into my comfy seat among the Hollywood A-listers when someone came and tapped Denny's shoulder. Denny cued me to stand and escorted me up the aisle away from the stage. Feeling mortified as I swished by Dustin Hoffman, like anyone would have known who I was, I thought we were being busted for seat-stealing, something I'd do at concerts in the old days hoping the actual ticket holders didn't show up.

It wasn't until afterward that I learned we were seat-fillers, which is a legit thing. The show producers have people on hand to fill the seats that people vacate, so when the camera pans the audience, it's always full. Denny knew the drill, of course, but neglected to clue me in.

An LA native, Denny was plugged-in and a man about town. He had a ton of connections and was the ultimate power networker. It may have helped that his brother, Steve, was a well-respected literary agent and traveled with the likes of then golden boy David E. Kelly.

Friendly, outgoing and talking to everyone, Denny made shit happen. For all those invitations he got for the Hollywood events he'd barter dresses, Mica dresses. He was doing product seeding and collabing way before the word "influencer" entered our modern-day vocabulary, which brings me to a point.

Make no mistake, everything we do today has its origin

in the way things have been done before, in fact, since the beginning of time. We just have different means to do it now. Weren't Jesus's apostles his brand ambassadors? Didn't he have a community of followers? You get the point.

I had the opportunity to not only help steer Mica's success but to learn from the best. One of the most valuable lessons came during a meeting with a stone-faced Macy's buyer. I accused her of having a chip on her shoulder when she didn't seem phased or interested as I was showing her the next hot major trend in fashion. Not my finest moment admittedly, and she proceeded to call Denny in LA and give him an earful about his NY rep, yours truly.

He navigated the situation with sniper precision and brought a meeting of the minds. And yes, she wrote the order. The lesson I learned, though, was in the words he told me, his incensed rep, in the midst of my "How dare she!" moment. He simply said these words, "The best revenge is selling them." I never asked Denny what he told her. But, I wonder as I write this if he told her the best revenge is buying from them. LOL.

Suffice to say the Macy's buyer and I got along from that point forward. And yes, if you're wondering, they blew out of the goods. The best revenge is selling them. It's become one of my favorite business tenets. Take the emotion out of it, get the order, and keep the train moving.

Mica would be the first of many brands that I'd launch out of the Times Two Showroom and this would be just one of the many lessons I'd learn along the way.

Above: My brother Chris and me

Below: My sister Maria and me

Right: My mom and me on my wedding
day in New York, circa 1985.
Silk satin, blush-colored gown.
Custom-made crown headpiece.

Rocking an early nineties Goth look.
Eye the boxy computer. Still no email yet.

Hello, '90s!
On the Move

Nearing the end of a killer decade, no one epitomized it more than mega star Madonna, who I had the opportunity to see in real life a number of times. The most dramatic was at The Supper Club with her entourage. As her grand table of twelve got up seemingly in unison, they all followed her out single file as she dragged her fur coat on the floor.

Madonna would indirectly impact my life again a couple of years later when my good friend Sally's live-in boyfriend dumped her for the hot pop star. The story we got was that Carlos met her in Central Park while riding his bicycle. It was drama central for a while, and things hit a fever pitch when Sally and her sister pinned Carlos at World Gym, cursing him out.

Madonna then called and left an intimidating message on Sally's home machine, which I had the pleasure of hearing. The funniest part was that Sally, who happened to be an aspiring singer, sampled part of the message as a beat in her next single. "Sally, this is Madonna." in a stern tone repeated over and over. Madonna and Carlos would later welcome a baby girl into the world and name her Lourdes.

A couple of years after that, one of her prominent backup dancers from the uber-famous Vogue video showed up with Fred at my birthday party. I got an earful about how all the dancers felt slighted after receiving no money to be in her Truth or Dare documentary. I fancied I had made it. A real insider.

It was a time when Marithé & Francois Girbaud ruled the streets with their signature yoke-front baggies in stone washed denim and outerwear like the leather shearling maxi coat Michele picked up in Montreal and still has to this day. LOL. The glitz and glam that we once heralded was slowly transitioning to a more understated vibe.

As the nineties came into focus, grunge pervaded from music to fashion. Think Nirvana and Marc Jacobs' controversial last collection for Perry Ellis. It was also a time of minimalism with the re-emergence of luxury heritage brand Prada, which was the first of many that led the decade.

Calvin Klein and Tom Ford for Gucci defined the times. And we first heard the term super model to describe the likes of Naomi Campbell, Linda Evangelista, and Christy Turlington, to name a few. And witnessed the radical rise of a five-foot seven Kate Moss who joined the ranks.

The impact of TV shows, such as *Friends* and *Sex and the City*, had a significant influence on fashion trends with characters' outfits becoming iconic and widely copied. *Friends* premiered and would become a cultural phenomenon with famous lines still resonating today like Ross' "We were on a break!" and the hairstyle known as "The Rachel" dubbed after the character.

But, *Sex and the City*, coming later in the decade launched certain brands into the stratosphere like Manolo Blahnik, whose heels were a fave of the main character Carrie. Funny story, I was shopping at Barneys with my puppy, Toby, when an excited Sarah Jessica Parker promptly fell to her knees to shower love on him and when I told her his name, she eagerly declared that Toby was her brother's name too. But, I digress. Another ascendent brand from the show was that of Fendi with their "baguette bag," which reached icon status and became a must-have after it was featured.

Seinfeld, though not known for its fashion, also debuted in the '90s and is widely regarded today as one of the greatest sitcoms of all time so it deserves inclusion. It featured famous lines such as "No soup for you!" It's interesting to think that all the hottest shows took place in my town, New York City.

Urban streetwear brands emerged as did sneaker culture and preppy fashion. The internet was hitting its stride with websites and email. Boy bands and platform shoes were a thing. And, it was the golden age of hip-hop.

It was also a time when I would heartbreakingly say goodbye to Richard. My overwhelming, inexpressible grief over losing my mother and big brother never left and had forced me to retreat emotionally. Instead of drawing closer to him for comfort, I took to eating away my deep sadness. Coupling that with my intermittent fits of hysteria and the demands of a new thriving business, I was detached in our relationship. He repeatedly tried to pull me back until he couldn't any longer and went back to Montreal.

I spent the first couple of days feeling disoriented and alone after things ended. But, like a flipped switch, it was game on, and I was back to the business at hand. I quickly learned that my deep drive and ambition could remedy any emotional upheaval I was feeling, at least at the time. Later in life, I came to understand that the only way out is through, and you have to feel it to heal it. But, that's a story for another time.

Eventually, pressing onward, I would spread out and take over Panos's whole showroom. I always got the sense that he came from family money because he clearly wasn't doing any business, and I remember being awestruck the day he unpacked the very first mobile phone I ever saw that weighed in at 2.5 pounds and looked like a big brick. So, as his "Fifteen days." became never, I was first in line to expand and take over the whole space, all 500 square feet. Yes, I started in a third of that space. Don't throw shade on humble beginnings.

In those days, it wasn't easy getting space in the building let alone the coveted fourth floor, which was impossible. Quickly outgrowing Panos's entire space, a lucky break came when the closed-door fabric rep, who was in the adjacent showroom, left the building.

The guy was an anomaly. First, he wasn't a fashion brand. And second, he was considerably older than all of us and didn't quite fit in with the open-door college dorm vibe that was the essence of the fourth floor. Endings for some are beginnings for others, and I was poised to continue expanding my budding empire.

Leading up to this, I would call Holly, the building leasing agent, to see if anyone was leaving, and I would regularly pop in at her office in the building. I was practically stalking her. Everyone wanted in, and being relatively new, I needed to make sure I would stake my claim and be first in line for the next spot that opened up. I can say with utmost confidence that the squeaky wheel does get the oil.

At more than double the size of my current space, it was a significant upgrade. I got a fresh blank slate to work with. Pulling back the dingy, gray wall-to-wall revealed cement floors, which I put a high gloss finish on.

I furnished it eclectically with local vintage finds. This was in the days of the famed 26th Street flea market that was the preeminent weekend spot to see and be seen with cool New Yorkers getting their vintage groove on. Don't bother looking for it today unless you need a place to live. The parking lot parcels that once housed some of the coolest shit on the planet gave way to high rise apartments. RIP 26th Street Flea.

Another trend-maker I'd launch out of the new space would be a young Natalie D. Fresh out of design school, her boho (before boho was even a thing) crocheted maxi vest and flared pants and other separates hit the scene with a splash. It was so forward that Saks Fifth Avenue wanted to feature her in a full-page New York Times ad and cover the total cost. That was virtually unheard of back then. Number one, to even get offered a full-page Times ad. And number two, not to be expected to pay for it. Suffice to say, it was a big deal. And co-branding with Saks elevated her profile, which for a young designer is everything.

You can imagine my surprise when I went to Natalie's factory in LA and saw they were making the bespoke crochet pieces out of tablecloths sourced from China. So imaginative, they managed to engineer the scalloped edges on the garments to give a decorative, intentional finish. I admire such ingenuity, which is just one reason I loved what I was doing. The thrill of experiencing new, innovative ideas and applications has always inspired me. It's the spark I continue to carry with me wherever I find myself.

Looking back, with its emotional and rocky start I had personally, the nineties still wound up being a killer decade. With the synchronicity of all that was happening in my world and the world at large, it was during those years that I solidified my place in fashion as an arbiter of style.

Hustle & Grind

always felt like we had escaped the soul-sucking corporate environments and found a means to make money in a cool, relaxed way that fostered individuality and creativity, though nothing was really relaxed. We hustled. We had to pull in the numbers for the brands.

One time, I even flew to LA in the morning and came back the same day just to land an order, a huge order. I had to be back in NY, but it's a get-'em-while-they're-hot business, and you do whatever it takes. Close the deal, get the order.

Seasonally, we'd participate in trade shows held at various hotels, the Piers, and the Javits Center. We'd practically take the whole showroom with us, including hundreds of garments, and we'd settle in for three to four days to work with out-of-town buyers. This was particularly grueling because we'd have to load in and out from our building and again at the venue with hundreds of other brands.

In the early days, at the Boutique Show, I'd have a long

row of booths to house all the labels. It was important that each one had its unique identity under the umbrella of the Times Two Showroom brand. Before each show, we'd brainstorm how we wanted our booths to appear visually, and we'd have to execute any set design to accomplish it.

Marie and George were this adorable rag-tag couple who ran around wearing baggy, paint-splattered clothes. With creativity dripping from them like the paint on their overalls, they made some of the most original booth displays, earning us best in show three times. Among them were the bespoke, hand-painted canvas backdrops with logos and landscapes that were visually stunning. These awards came from trade event producer, the Larkin Group, and we'd receive a wooden and metal engraved plaque to show for it.

People swarmed the booths to buy, while others, like people from the leadership team at Urban Outfitters, would literally just stand there and stare, seemingly awestruck, trying to identify what compelled the crowd. All of this, coupled with the massive volume of orders we'd take home, put me on top of the world. Ahh, the glory days.

One such time, our mover bailed on us at the last minute. We were faced with the dilemma of getting close to eight hundred garments, rolling racks, display props, mannequins, signage, file cabinets and office supplies, all back to our showroom. It was a daunting task, so you can imagine how lucky we felt to find another mover loitering outside.

Since we didn't know them and wanted to make sure

they didn't drive off with all our stuff, we rode back with them to our building. This was NYC after all, couldn't be too trusting. And as they started to unload the lines out of the truck, we went up to the showroom.

We were waiting and waiting, but no one came. When we saw our other fourth floor besties, who were also loading in, we asked them if they had seen the mover. One said they saw someone loading clothes back into their truck.

You guessed it. Still in market week after the show, we had to make the dreaded call to each one of the brands to tell them their collections had been heisted, and we needed them replaced stat. Good times.

But, I learned a very big lesson that day, to trust my instincts. I had a feeling someone should wait with them while they loaded the collections into the freight elevator. I voiced my concerns but was swayed by an employee, who was also a friend. I'm sure she didn't want to be the one left waiting. Thanks, Lisa. Note to self: trust your gut, it doesn't lie.

Lisa couldn't have been with me for more than six or eight months, but she taught me a lot. She was my sales rep when I was a buyer, and after Richard and I split up, we cultivated a friendship, having reconnected when by coincidence we were both traveling in Greece and met up there.

After her first couple of months on the job, she approached me saying she felt entitled to being made a partner. Seriously?, I thought. You gotta be kidding me. Little did I know, she would go on to scheme behind my back and cut deals with a couple of my weakest lines to go open her own showroom and take them with her.

One brand in particular that wasn't entirely embracing the current trends, had an owner that called us daily, and she would badmouth them every time. She took him, and with her encouragement and direction, he created a new brand that went head-to-head with my hottest line.

The lesson here? First off, never hire friends. It's hard to go out for drinks one night being all jolly, and then the next day, manage them and tell them what to do. Blurry lines cause resentments. Second lesson, well, no second lesson. I said it's a dog-eat-dog industry, and shit like this happens all the time.

Movin' On Up

Cut to 1992, the year George Michaels' "Too Funky" music video wowed viewers with a parade of supermodels vogueing the runway. Outgrowing the space once again, as scaling businesses do, I made my big move down the hall to the coveted, huge corner showroom. Once inhabited by an uber successful rep named Susan, the spot had some seriously good juju. Aside from having great lines, Susan's other claim to fame was her big lawsuit win after she sued a brand for not paying her commission. Gotta love a badass.

With the help of Marie and George, we created an experience, not a showroom. The grand entryway still had vestiges of the original Terrazzo tile floor, which we would find hidden beneath the wall-to-wall carpet. The rest of the floor was cement and the space had fourteen-foot ceilings.

I was so inspired by the loftiness that my big design spark came when I envisioned installing casement windows along the upper back wall that concealed our offices from the rest of the showroom. The light lover I am, I wanted to make sure the brightness from the huge Broadway-facing windows could radiate through, while even more light flowed through the windows all along West 42nd Street.

Fully embracing a gothic moment, we had custom-designed wrought iron racks that were overbearing and elaborate with their various scroll details and candy cane twisted rods accented with finials. Coordinating curtain rods flaunted wine-colored crushed velvet drapes that pooled on the painted cement floors.

Marie and George did an amazing job replicating the Terrazzo pattern to resemble broken away tiles throughout the massive space. Wrought iron tables with cabriole legs and glass tops, ornate show bars where we presented the collections, and slipcovered taupe brocade slipper chairs completed the look. Chairs were intentionally extra cushy, and the buyers didn't want to leave.

The imaginative duo also created an entryway harlequin pattern on the wall in muted taupes and beiges, in front of which sat two ornately carved Gothic ebony wood throne chairs with deep red velvet seats. Thanks, 26th St. Flea. This showroom was trend-setting in its look and feel as were the collections I represented. The big reveal told the world Times Two had entered a new paradigm.

The Brand Maker

My showroom was a must-stop shop for every savvy retailer, large and small, looking for the next hot trends in fashion. Editors for all the magazines dropped by and called out styles regularly for their meetings. I recall a young, wide-eyed Rachel Zoe coming in from time to time when she was an assistant editor at the now defunct YM magazine. She went by her full name back then, Rachel Rosenzweig.

Hot celebs of the moment, like Mariah Carey and Marisa Tomei, came with their stylists to shop. Up-and-coming retail superstars, like Intermix, made their humble beginnings when co-founder Khajak frequented the showroom and did the buying himself. At the time, he had only one store on Long Island called Trendmix.

Keep in mind, in the early days, there was no internet, so no e-commerce, only physical retail stores and direct mail catalogs. The only way to get a brand out there was to sell to brick and mortar stores and catalogs or open your own. My showroom acted as the liaison between the brands and the retailers. Back then, a showroom could make or break your business as a brand.

We showed the collections and pulled in the orders and sent them to the brands to manufacture and ship to the retailers. It was so early that in the very beginning we mailed in the orders because there weren't even fax machines yet! LOL.

Even funnier, we had to buy these big published volumes, think chunky yellow pages, that had all the big buyers listed with their phone numbers and we'd have to cold call them. There was no email. Fun times!

Brands could try and sell on their own to the stores, but it wasn't easy. Many times, if they were just starting they didn't really understand the business and what the retailer's expectations were. Even today, for those wanting to go the wholesale route, new entrants often don't understand branding and product positioning. As a result, they don't know which stores to sell and which ones not to sell, what to say and what not to say, if they even get a meeting.

Many retailers don't want to work with start-up brands. They prefer to wait it out a couple of seasons to see how the brand develops, unless it's so radically amazing that they lust over it. Only if you possess what I've come to call "musthaveness" can you get in from the start. This entails the buyer's perception that you are so cutting edge that they want to be first to market or you're capitalizing on an uber-relevant trend in a new, compelling way or one they're already retailing. All told, they essentially must have you.

The showrooms, on the other hand, have established

relationships with the buyers. So, their representation adds street cred and signals that your brand is worthy of attention. As a showroom, we built a core customer base, whom we were completely dialed into, only taking in lines we felt would be right for them.

They became our barometer, and any constructive feedback we received we communicated to our designers. This helps to improve and shape a brand. If you're in the wrong showroom, one that is misaligned with your brand, and they don't have the right buyers, the feedback you get can be very misleading.

Also integral to the success of Times Two was the kick-ass sales and management team, many of whom went on to create their own businesses, which makes me immensely proud. Though, part of me wonders if they collectively thought, I'll never work for someone again.

Let's just say I had my *Devil Wears Prada* moments in those days. I can still remember the bewildered look on one employee's face when I read them the riot act for bringing the wrong milk for my coffee. Not my finest moment. But, I'd rather think they watched and learned how to run a successful company during their tenure. Ok, maybe it was a little of both?

Kathy, who was one of my brilliant hires, ran the sales team and incidentally later opened her own showroom in Los Angeles. She had been my sales rep when I was a buyer, so she was a seasoned pro. Knowing sales were being diligently managed under her watchful eye gave me more time to personally sit with the brand owners and designers to help them focus on their product offerings. What was good, what was bad, what they needed more of.

Assisting them with design, I offered my input on specific elements to add to the line. For example, if they were introducing a new textile, I might have some ideas for new silhouettes. Or I might tell them about a type of fabric I believed in that they should source or a seasonal color I felt was important. I also helped them identify new opportunities in the market and possible product extensions.

I offered my expertise in editing and merchandising the collection, too. Editing is a critical component to any successful line. I see the ideal collection as art. Envision a mass of stone and, as we chisel away, a beautiful sculpture reveals itself. In fashion, we do this by first taking out extraneous pieces in the collection. These are outliers and don't feel like they belong. Then, we look for any styles that appear redundant and would split sales, ultimately.

Rather than competing, pieces should enhance one another and all sing the same song. The goal is to create a tight, cohesive collection with a strong and concise POV. A well-edited collection exudes confidence and compels attention.

If you are creating a capsule group with five styles, you might want a jacket, a pant, two tops – a cami and a long-sleeve blouse – and a dress. Each piece has a reason for being, and there is nothing superfluous that would split sales. You might say that it's well-edited and merchandised. On the other hand, you could have a collection with various groups in the same delivery, and the way pieces are pulled out and cross-coordinated among them to create new looks is also considered merchandising.

I routinely provided guidance and support for the brands, helping to elevate them. I showed them the ropes. Through these close working relationships and the successful launches and growth of many brands, my credibility and visibility continued to increase, and I eventually opened a second showroom in Los Angeles.

I was contacted by several hundred brands over the course of ten years. A select few were chosen to be accepted into the showroom. I gave lots of advice along the way. Even the brands that weren't right for my showroom, I always tried to point them in the right direction and give them my honest feedback and a couple helpful tips. I built a reputation for being tough but honest and forthright.

Not everyone was ready for the big leagues, though. It was a time when cottage industry brands entered the vernacular. These were scrappy start-ups that in many cases got press but their volume didn't match the level of their cool factor and hype.

I recall one such brand that was really onto something. They were a twentysomething hipster couple doing pastel-colored terry cloth separates. Might sound lame now, but they were directional at the time.

I took them in, but when I got a huge order for them, they were like deer in the headlights, trying and failing to produce such a large quantity. I'll never forget the day I had to gently tell them I could no longer represent them.

After all, my reputation was on the line, too. No pun intended. When I represented a brand, I was giving it instant credibility in the eyes of the buyer. I felt so bad and so did they. I'll never forget the heartbroken look in their eyes.

The irony of having success as a fashion brand rep is that the more volume you do for a brand, the more you are at risk of losing them. After you've launched them to the world like a debutante at her ball, there comes a time when most brands feel it's the next right step to leave the nest and open their own corporate showroom. Thank you for putting me on the map, see ya.

This usually happens because they need a more dedicated sales team as they are scaling. Or they want to solidify their brand identity on their own. And many times, it's because the financial heads come in and say, "You are paying too much for sales by being in a commissioned showroom, and it's negatively affecting your bottom line." So, one by one, the brands whose hands I held and growth I nurtured exited the showroom.

Remember Mica? They broke up with me after three years when I was in Paris with another designer shopping stores. Brands were contacting me pretty much on the daily, and I started working more closely with the ones that were open to my feedback and held the most promise. But, little by little, as I brought in other brands, I knew Denny & Judy felt they were losing my full attention. Like scorned lovers, they ended the relationship in a "Fuck you!" way.

I always gave Mica my all, not entirely recognizing the potential detriment to my business if they left. They were my biggest revenue driver. This is known as concentration. Business 101: You should never find yourself with all or most of your revenue coming from one source.

With nearly seventy percent of my revenue gone in one fell swoop, as soon as I returned from Paris, I boarded a flight to LA to scout for new lines. This felt familiar because just like when I was a buyer, most contemporary brands were still based there. Susan from our foursome, was the head buyer for Cignal, the trendy retail chain at the time. She made some intros, so I would hit the ground running with scheduled meetings, all in downtown LA.

As soon as I left for the airport, I realized I had forgotten to bring my business cards. In those days, business cards really meant something. If you showed up in a business environment without one, it spoke to an utter lack of professionalism. Suffice to say, they were uber important to have. Panicked, I quickly called my sister to have her track mine down and overnight some to me. Crisis averted! Thanks, Maria.

Alas, that was the life of an independent sales rep. Losing Mica was a hard but vital lesson that taught me to never get too comfortable with my brand mix and always keep my eyes and ears open for the next big thing. Nothing is forever. Discretion is key, though, because if the brands suspect you're doing that, they become like jealous boyfriends. Sooo, it's a Catch-22.

But, introducing brands into the market and building them into hot commodities was my sole purpose for having my showroom, and I did it with great success.

Times Two Showroom, circa 1994

Hello, Los Angeles!
One Door Closes
& Many Open

When I arrived in LA, I set out to meet with several brands. With some, you can intuitively feel a synergy, while with others, not so much. On my checklist was, first and foremost, the product. It had to meet the following criteria. Is it fresh looking? Do I believe in it and can I sell it to my stores? Is the company organized and shipping a quality product on time that fits?

Fit is hyper-critical. You can have the most beautiful, relevant designs, but if the fit isn't good or the quality is off, you're done. It's very hard to come back from that once the first impression is made.

Other important things to consider that were on my list... Is the company funded to be able to produce high volume? We had all the customers, and the ability to get large orders so this was key. Do I get a sense they have integrity? Bear in mind we were only paid commission on what shipped, and usually 30-45 days after. Will they sign our contract that stipulates, among other things, that we are entitled to be paid on 85% of the credit approved orders we submit, whether they ship or not? This protected us because we invested time and money to get the orders, and we needed to be compensated. Are they amenable to feedback and actioning on suggestions in a timely manner? That's a big one.

As a rep, I was on the front line, presenting the collections and working with the buyers. I got to feel the product and notice any holes – things that were missing or didn't work. It was vital to communicate any constructive buyer feedback to the brands, as well. The information I was able to glean was invaluable. Continuous collaboration with the buyers and brands was key to bringing the best product to the market.

Sometimes, the lines that seemed cool and edgy could be a train wreck, so it was automatically a no-go. We had a reputation to uphold. On the other hand, there were brands with collections that might not be earth-shaking, but the product was solid and the company organized, well-funded and seemed to act with integrity. These brands were definitely worth my consideration.

One such brand was Michi Collection. Upon entering their headquarters, which consisted of multiple floors in a factory building downtown, I immediately picked up on a sense of professionalism. They were a company that meant business.

I first met with the designer, who appeared amiable and competent as she showed me her mood boards and a collection of primarily soft-colored stretch lace. She then proceeded to give me a tour of the place, during which we ran into the owner who struck me funny because she didn't possess the usual profile of an LA fashion founder. Instead, she looked like someone who stepped out of an estate in Connecticut, spearheaded benefit dinners and rode horses.

So, you can only imagine my astonishment when I gazed around me and the production happening before my eyes was that of primary-colored, exotic dancewear. This was their main business, which they sold direct-to-consumer through a printed catalog.

I was invited to the owner's office to talk business. As we made our way, I followed her and the German shepherd by her side into an industrial private elevator. My subsequent dealings with Michi would remain as professional as our first meeting. They even sent me a fax to tell me they were leaving the showroom, no phone call.

Above: Pitstop at a Paris café on a shopping trip with Natalie D, circa 1993. Guy in the pic is unknown. LOL.

Below: Denny & me on our way to the Oscars, leaving from his factory. Of course, he had me wearing a Mica dress. LOL.

Teamwork Makes
the Dream Work

ith some brands, it was all formal business. In other cases, we just clicked and could groove together and make magic happen. One such meeting that held great promise was with the brand NC17. They were a family-run business with the oldest brother, Albert, as their very charismatic leader. I think his Dad had started the business selling in the famed Santee Alley. Eventually, I'd meet his younger siblings, Joe and Danielle.

Albert, who sported sterling silver necklaces and artisanal beaded bracelets, epitomized LA cool at the time. With his healthy, Mediterranean, tanned glow and thick head of wavy hair, I sensed he took great pride in his appearance.

Fully engaged as we conversed, he intently leaned forward on his desk, which seemed kind of big for his stature, as I remember it. We immediately hit it off. I think he respected my business acumen, deep knowledge of product and my connections with all the right buyers.

Plus, I had just blown-up Mica in my showroom, so my reputation preceded me.

We took our convo to dinner that night, where he was intent on getting underneath my authoritative business demeanor to understand who I really was. With a penetrating look, he asked, "What's your story?" I found this funny, and it broke through my strong veneer to uncover the spark that would ignite not only a mutually lucrative working relationship but also a close friendship.

At the time, his line pretty much had two styles. But, not just any two styles. These rang the register and reordered immediately every time they hit the selling floor. Both were in the same fabric, broomsticked poly in assorted ditsy prints. This was a crinkle process done after the styles were sewn. One was a bohemian dirndl style maxi skirt and the other a buttoned-front cap sleeved maxi dress. Both personified the grunge trend that was emerging.

We got to work right away expanding the collection. What I loved was Albert's ability to execute on a dime. I'd send over a sketch or a body to knock off, and in two days a sample would be in my showroom in NY. He gave me the freedom to unlock my inner designer.

I had glimpses of this when I created private label programs as a buyer and then again at Mica. It's true what they say. When others are made a part of the process, it's more likely they'll take ownership in working toward a common goal. I learned that firsthand. With Albert, my input was welcomed and executed on, which motivated me all the more to sell the shit out of the line.

I traveled to LA frequently. And on one of my visits, I

was sitting in Albert's huge office, which I'll dub Control Central, where all the right and left brain masterminding took place, when a fabric supplier interrupted us, and for good reason. He was bringing strike-offs in for approval of the prints that Albert bought for the broomstick pieces, one of which wasn't matching the color standards that had been submitted.

It was both not horrible and not great. The majority of designers would have rejected it. But, not Albert. He looked at me and, knowing I'd want an explanation, said, "While everyone is going back and forth, I'm shipping goods." Translation: Don't major in minor things, and perfection is the enemy of execution.

This is gold, and I've carried it with me through the years. Many times, as creators, we get something that wasn't what we anticipated. If we let go of the expectations we had and look at it for what it is, we can find the beauty in it. And in many cases, it even turns out better. A lesson for life, too.

Albert also exhibited a fearlessness in business. Along with that must come a subconscious trust that everything will be alright in the end, no matter what. Even though the risks were far greater, he thrived on big orders. The bigger the better. And, never indecisive, he made decisions quickly and succinctly.

"Just because you bought a rotten fish doesn't mean you have to eat it." was one of his sage adages. And I've found that to be true over the years. It's better to cut your losses and move on than to continue with something that isn't proving worthwhile, even if you've invested time, money and effort. Albert came from an abundance mindset, always trusting better things were in store.

He also had the innate ability to surround himself with people who knew the things he didn't. I admired that in him. As an entrepreneur, if you're the smartest person in the room, you're in the wrong room. Assessing and identifying key talent to drive growth is an art and one that he did well. Heck, he chose me. LOL.

As the brand continued to blow up, I would eventually accompany him to London to meet with a potential distributor for Europe. We also went to Paris a few times to shop for prints at Première Vision, the international fabric show. I remember the excitement of seeing the silver pony tail of Karl Lagerfeld as he glided up the extraordinarily long escalator in the Parc des Expositions.

Forever the brainstormers, we were always looking for an angle to keep us from getting too complacent with the success we were having and to stay ahead of the competition. Albert's brother, Joe, had a friend with access to truckloads of vintage and presented an opportunity where Albert would pay for a truckload, and Joe's friend would design into it. Today, this is widespread and known as upcycling.

After we convened, Albert gave Joe's friend the go-ahead to get the vintage and start re-imagining the pieces. He'd work out of the building on a lower floor. About a day later, he knocked on the door of Control Central with his first creation.

When we saw his face, we looked at each other and immediately cracked up. The business was so fast-paced with so much going on creatively and otherwise, we had moved on and totally forgotten about him and the whole situation. Still makes me laugh to this day.

Joe was the complete opposite of Albert. He was a free-spirited, long-haired, young, twentysomething hippie who wore grungy clothes and seemed to bathe only on odd days. He smoked copious amounts of weed and was a gentle, soulful man with vulnerability in his eyes that could be seen beyond his wire rimmed grandad spectacles. He would quietly saunter into Control Central, kind of lean his lanky frame on the side of Albert's desk and listen to the conversation already in play.

I would come to learn that creativity came intuitively and naturally to Joe, like breathing. He previously had a men's line that garnered lots of press and booked like a million and a half dollars at his first trade show. A wunderkind, Joe was and is a true visionary designer. Contrary to what you might think, these are few and far between in fashion.

Even though I would come to grow a formidable fashion brand on my own, it's always been lonely at the top. I always felt I was slightly better as part of a team, a worker among workers. The sparking of ideas and bouncing off one another pushes and invites you to see beyond the confines of your own mind.

Having the opportunity to collaborate with Albert and Joe and other great minds in fashion, witnessing their genuine artistry in action, has offered me some of the highest points in my career. To come across those who brought out the best in me and I in them is the true essence of a winning collaboration.

On the phone, as usual, in my baby tee
and slip dress, circa 1992

A Trend is Born

This next part may seem controversial, and to this day, I can't say I'd do it any differently. But, around the same time, I was repping a brand called Tease Tees, the original baby tee developed by a Hollywood stylist. This was a shrunken short sleeve t-shirt that looked like it was for your little sister with a white elastic exposed neckband.

I vividly remember the buyers looking skeptically at the prepubescent, little tees as I strongly encouraged them to give a test order. Seeing the opportunity before me when we first started selling the tees, I knew this was going to blow the fuck up.

The founder, was brand new to the game and was moving very slowly, snail-like. I remember excitedly telling her, "We need more colors, long sleeves, maybe add a dress, change the elastic color perhaps!" and I was met with the low-energy LA response of, "Well, maybe I can add a long sleeve in the next couple of months."

Fashion moves fast and you have to strike while the iron

is hot. If I hadn't gotten this done, another brand with another rep would have jumped on it. That's the way it is.

News travels fast in this industry, and people hop on the bandwagon. Why do you think you see a certain trend, and all of a sudden, everyone is doing it? We are cannibals when it comes to product in this industry. Nothing is sacred. Anyone can knock off another designer's silhouette with little to no recourse. We're talking Wild West, baby.

I shared my frustration about the situation with Albert, communicating that I knew this was going to be the next trend to explode. Within maybe a couple of weeks I had the first collection of baby tees that was named Joes. It blew away the original tee.

There were cool in-house designed screen-prints and a vast array of garment-dyed colors, short and long sleeves. There were even amazing knits inspired by the prolific Parisian brand, Xuly Bet to round out the collection. The rest became history.

We paired the baby tees with maxi slip dresses from NC17. Just throw on a knit cap, and tie a plaid flannel shirt around your hips. And don't forget the Doc Martens. The nineties grunge uniform brought to you by Times Two Showroom.

The baby tee trend, especially, was a particularly fascinating product study. It was the first and only time I've seen a single item being sold at exactly the same time to stores from luxury retailer Barneys to the likes of junior chain Contempo Casuals and everyone in between.

Another hot item from NC17, emerging around this time, rayon floral-printed bias cut skirts, secured million-dollar orders from notables, such as Victoria's Secret & Limited Express. We'd later take trips down to their campus in Columbus, Ohio to work with the buyers developing other product. We were given a tour of their humongous warehouse and introduced to their fully automated fulfillment process which was cutting edge at the time.

Along the way, having key items, as we call them, can ignite movements.

But, lots goes on behind the scenes before it ends up in someone's closet. Our things were seen on culturally relevant movies and TV shows, like *Clueless* and *Friends*. Before they got there, they all started somewhere.

"New" and "trend forward" had become synonymous with my showroom and that continually attracted all the buyers, stylists, and press. Consistently being first-to-market and a trend-maker had its privileges. Suffice to say we made LOTS of money.

All mega fashion trends start somewhere, and for many throughout the '90s in the US, I was fortunate enough to be an integral part of their development, launch and success.

Above: Albert & me at the Boutique Show

Left: The dawn of the baby tee. Early days
of Coterie, flaunting my wares.

Coterie in the old days at the Plaza Hotel, circa 1993

Set up day at the Boutique Show, circa 1993.
Eye the canvas mural by Marie & George.

Retail Comeback

By the mid-nineties, while having a strong core group of brands that were selling well, I decided to open a retail store called Unchained on Amsterdam and 80th Street to showcase these and other brands I'd curate and buy from the market. I settled on the name for reasons I can't remember, though I do recall the logo included a rendering of Liberty Leading the People by Delacoix brought to you by none other than Marie and George. Unleashing their unwavering creativity on the store, we had Klimt-inspired murals and mosaic-tiled custom shelving and a cash wrap to coordinate.

At the core of the assortment were Joes and NC17, which was later changed to NC Love after receiving a cease and desist letter from the Motion Picture Association. They should have seen that coming.

I loved that I got to reprise my role as retail buyer. The act of buying always made me feel like I was a kid in a candy store. Tasty and fun! I roved around the trade shows we participated in, viewing collections and extracting the best items. With a thriving showroom of my own to run, my time was limited. So, I had to get it all done without the luxury of visiting showrooms.

The store was conveniently located around the block from where I lived and was managed by my sister, Maria. My long-time dream had finally become a reality. I got to pop in on the weekends and listen to customer feedback, which I always found fascinating. And I loved cashing people out at the register.

Old habits die hard. Forever the merchant. It harkens back to the days when I helped my dad at the grocery store, making change out of the cigar box on the counter I could barely see over. I was way too little to reach and operate the ornate brass cash register.

Although it was a dream come true, I remember feeling very stretched between having a retail store and a thriving showroom. I felt like I had no personal life and was living to work rather than working to live. So, after a year and a fifty-thousand-dollar profit, I decided to switch gears.

I figured if I was going to hustle the return on investment had to be way more than that 50k. Bear in mind, making a profit after one year is pretty good, and we would have built it up. But, I had my sights set on greener pastures with far greater upsides.

Halcyon Days

Repping NC Love & Joes accounted for some of the best times I've had in my career. My team and I were all twenty and early thirtysomethings who had life by the balls. We played hard and worked harder. We traveled to foreign cities, stayed in trendy hotels, ate the best food, drank fine wine and champagne and usually threw back a dirty martini or two.

On one such trip, Kathy and I went to London Fashion Week to see our friend Tina's incredible show. We stayed at Claridge's, where I had a deep talk in the lobby bar with Keanu Reeves about what it takes to be in fashion and shared pleasantries in the hotel elevator with Angelica Huston. The cherry on top was Kathy and I hanging out with Spike Lee at Momo's, dancing the night away. So many great memories!

We did a ton of tradeshows and market weeks through the years in New York, Miami, Las Vegas, Los Angeles, Atlanta, Dallas, and Paris. The trade shows, especially, had an energy and life sorely missed today. Back in the early days, in times when the economy was booming and the only places to shop were brick-and-mortar retail stores, there were a lot more buyers floating around.

I fondly remember one time when we were doing the Boutique show, and New York got hit with a severe snowstorm, dubbed the Blizzard of '96. We figured no one could get to the show over at the Javits, so we found our way to the Ziegfeld Theater to watch 12 Monkeys, with Joe leading the charge. That was so much fun. Good times!

Looking back, there was excitement and possibility and always the promise of the next big trend or great adventure... But, as they say, all good things must come to an end, and it finally did with NC Love & Joes. Our parting was emotional and drawn out, as such things can be when you work so closely and friendships are involved.

It marked the end of an era that is forever stamped in my mind. It's so easy not to recognize when you are at the top of your game. It wasn't the first nor would it be the last, that those moments would be lost on me.

The Next Frontier

few other brands sustained the business after the big parting. Among them was one-hit wonder Earl Jean that blew up after they were featured on the editorial back page of Vogue. A single page that carried clout within the industry, it highlighted brands other than the luxury designers that buy ad space and get the bulk of the editorial pages. It got them into stores like Bergdorf Goodman. I remember having around eight pairs of one jean on a table in the showroom in denim blue and white. An example of the power of an item.

And then there was Custo Barcelona, looking to launch in the US. Custo, the designer, had this massive collection. But, the uniquely printed tees were the item the stores were gravitating toward. It was a big pill for him to swallow and understand that the buyers had spoken. I encouraged them to run with that concept and they did all over the US and beyond and came to open several retail stores.

By this time, although having a showroom had afforded me a privileged lifestyle, I was over the hustle of repping. I grew tired of helping to build these brands with no equity stake. It really felt like a baby had left the nest when these lines went corporate. I immersed myself so deeply into these companies that retailers over and over were surprised to learn I had no ownership in them. But then again, that always was my work ethic, even when I worked for others on my come up. Their business became my business.

There used to be an Allstate commercial with the tagline, "Get a piece of the rock." I found myself wanting that, and so I decided to launch Alice & Trixie. My line, my baby, my piece of the rock.

My sister always liked to remind me that she came up with the name. It's still a bit foggy, but I believed her. They were the wives in the beloved fifties sitcom *The Honeymooners.*

It always made me chuckle when people asked where the name came from. When I'd tell them, they'd smile knowingly and say, "Ahhhh, yes." as they fondly remembered the show. Truth be told, my favorite old-time sitcom was the iconic *I Love Lucy.* But, the names Lucy & Ethel just didn't cut it. LOL. Alice & Trixie were much prettier and saying them together had a better ring to it.

Each stop on the fashion continuum taught me so much and gave me lifelong insights. Most of what I know to be successful in fashion I first learned on the retail selling floor – working with customers, then through leading a team, curating and buying brands, and doing private label product development. Selling brands wholesale while working intimately with the manufacturers to develop their labels and scale their businesses filled in the rest.

It had all prepared me well. So, with my mind made up and the name set, I was now ready to be at the helm of my own fashion brand as CEO & Creative Director.

OG Alice & Trixie
lover, Paris Hilton

Alice & Trixie is Born

t was 1997, the year Elton John paid tribute to Princess Diana with his number one hit, "Candle in the Wind." Bootstrapping once again, I started the company with $150,000 of my own hard-earned money, which incidentally was exactly one hundred times what I started Times Two with.

I did this for two reasons. One, to have working capital and two, so I could procure a factor. This is a sort of financial institution that can help you by advancing money on your confirmed purchase orders from buyers so you have the necessary cash flow to make the product until you get paid.

In those days, stores that had credit could delay paying you for thirty to sixty days on average. If you had no capital to start with, a factor wouldn't consider working with you at all. Being well-funded, I didn't do it for the usual reason, to get advances against my orders. I did it for another reason that I'd learned sitting outside of Soly's office for three years.

Once or twice a week, I witnessed the bookkeeper dropping on his desk a huge pile of invoices with checks to be signed, and always at the top were the factors. The factors got paid first, because if you didn't pay them on time you were effectively risking your credit standing with all the other brands that used that factor. Between that and knowing already that stores can dilly dally on payment, I wanted to make sure we got paid first. It also gave clout to your brand that you were big or important or serious enough to have one.

Being brand new to the game, I didn't know the first thing about where to go in New York to have patterns made or fabrics cut and sewn. A couple of friends, Nick and Nelly, had started their line two years earlier. So, I asked them for any guidance they could give me. They sat with me once and gave me a few resources. I sensed they weren't offering me anything too in-depth, lest I become their competition later.

Those days seemed a lot more competitive, and the industry was more concealed and had its trade secrets. Some say it's still like that. But, the conversation we had that day was just enough to make my beginning. Thank you, Nick and Nelly.

I remember having an irrational fear that the cutting room could potentially cut two left legs, wasting my fabric. I stayed away from pants in the beginning. I came up with some other ideas and set out to make my first patterns.

Sketches in hand, I walked over to the pattern service Nick recommended. The place was west of 8th Avenue in one of the stodgy factory buildings I remembered going into as a buyer all those years ago. Once inside the space, I found myself in a large workroom amongst a slew of dressmaker mannequins draped with muslin in various stages of completion and several patternmakers busily working away at their respective tables.

Looking back, I'm sure I had green written all over my forehead. Even though I had been exposed to the design and manufacturing process through the years, I still felt like a newbie. Looking out over the sea of people, one person stood out. For some reason, I could tell she knew more. She exuded confidence, even though she barely spoke English. I'd come to learn that her name was Linda.

Finally, patterns in hand, I was ready to have my first samples made. I can't remember how we found the sample sewer. But, I do remember the samples coming back so poorly sewn they couldn't be shown to buyers. Utterly disappointed, heading home that night, I had no idea what I was going to do.

Going through the subway turnstile by my office, after inserting my token (Yes, this was way before metrocards.), I looked up to find Linda, the confident patternmaker, walking toward me. I could barely understand her English but what came through was, "I want work for you." Thinking I was in the deep end of the pool, I gave her my business card and told her to come to my office to talk to me.

The very next day, she showed up and presented me with a bag of pork dumplings. Yum. The decision was made on the spot to hire her and not just because of the dumplings. Wink, wink.

Since hiring a patternmaker hadn't been on my to-do list that day and I now found myself with one, we unexpectedly needed a work space. So, we swiftly converted my cherished corner office into a design room. After clearing off my desk, which included moving my phone, a huge, boxy monitor, big-ass Rolodex, and tons of files, we laid down a large piece of plywood. And voila! We had a pattern table. Whatever it takes, I thought.

We ordered a dressmaker mannequin and Linda got busy draping and patternmaking. The rest became history. She would end up not only making patterns but running my sampling and coordinated production for the next seven years.

I always had one or more full-time, in-house patternmakers after that. What a luxury it was. Any idea executed at once. The first year, we experimented a lot, mostly trying different fabrics and silhouettes until we found our groove. It was easy since we had customers already coming to the showroom to see our other lines. Their consistent feedback helped shape the brand.

Along with all the specialty stores, we sold to accounts like Urban Outfitters, Anthropologie and Barneys, for whom we did private label based on my relationships with the buyers. This gave us a lift in our first year that brought us to $750K. Breaking even and feeling like I failed, I was distraught and called Albert. I remember him saying that maybe manufacturing wasn't for me.

It isn't for everyone. It's a hell of a lot riskier than repping brands. As a sales rep, you are effectively pushing paper. Show the line, get the order and send it to the brand to produce and ship. In manufacturing, there is much more stress and financial risk involved. It's not for the faint of heart. I vividly remember Albert once telling me that as soon as I faxed him an order, my job was done, and his nightmare began.

But thankfully, I forged ahead, undeterred, digging deep within myself to access the strength to persevere. Sometimes, you just have to have that moment of weakness, feel it, and then carry on. I hadn't come this far to drop the ball and run at the first sign of adversity. And perceived adversity at that.

I came to learn that breaking even in your first year of business is actually considered a success. I went on to double the volume in the second year, making a healthy profit, as well. The takeaway for me? Always trust and believe in yourself, and don't let other people's opinions discourage you. Had I taken Albert's words to heart, Alice & Trixie would have never taken off.

231 loft during construction

The Next Right Move

With Alice & Trixie gaining momentum, we began to phase out the repping and knew it was time to move to a new space. Our lease was almost up, anyway, and it was apparent that I needed my private office back and more space to warehouse the clothes we made. It was also no longer sustainable to ship out of the showroom with boxes all spread about on shipping days. There were other functions we needed space for, as well, now that we were a full-fledged fashion brand.

The building was shifting, too, and we were at the forefront of a showroom movement to the side streets when we were tapped to help pioneer 231 West 39th St. The timing was perfect for the next stage we were entering. At half the price, the building had a cool factor that 1466 lacked, even though 1466 had its merits. It was formally the renowned Knickerbocker Hotel built by American business magnate John Astor IV, who, as fate would have it, died in the sinking of the Titanic. And rumor had it that the opera great Enrico Caruso inhabited my space.

Another upside of 1466 was that we had the best vantage point on the fourth floor to view the Macy's Thanksgiving Day parade that marched by with its huge floats at eye level. Now, that was surreal, seeing them blowing in the wind as they made their way through the Broadway corridor between buildings, practically bouncing off our windows. I hosted annual parties and invited family and friends. We reveled in being high above the masses in a warm cozy space, drinking hot coffee and eating bagels, lox, and cream cheese.

Alas, that was all behind me now as I envisioned myself sashaying across the wooden plank floors in my cool, new loft space, wearing platforms. Yes, I was always wearing platforms and a maxi dress in my daydreams. I relished the thought of being a brand owner. Finally, design what I want, when I want.

The queen of my domain. Let the creative juices flow.

Our new, inspired space was a floor-through loft in a factory building that was converting as leases were running out, an omen for things to come with more and more production moving overseas. Grandfathered in at the low price with a full buildout paid for by the landlord to boot, my instinct to move there proved to be spot on because, after only a couple of years, the building became a must-stop shop just like 1466 was. Our further advantage was we could do all functions within one space under my watchful eye, except for bulk cutting and sewing, which we outsourced.

As fate would have it, the cutting room that did our

bulk production runs was located on the fifth floor and didn't leave during the mass exodus of these trades from the building. A lingerer from the old guard, Mr. Ma, or Ma as I called him, was a dedicated, hard worker hailing from China who presented a gruff exterior at first. But, hidden beneath resided a sweet guy who liked fishing and dogs, too, I'd discover.

His charm really came out when I brought Toby, my Jack Russell terrier, with me. Ma's cutting room would become a makeshift doggy daycare when I'd leave Toby there for hours. The funniest part was when I'd show up unexpectedly during lunch time to find the lights dimmed and the workers napping on the cutting tables with Toby sleeping beside them.

Heralding a new chapter in our growth, the building and the space served our needs well, so well we'd stay for the next eight years.

The Rise of Alice & Trixie

Looking back, the right people appeared at the right time, like angels swirling around me. I already had my patternmaker, sales were locked in, and bookkeeping was running smoothly.

I still needed help with operations and would make a versatile hire with Barry, who was in between higher profile gigs. He rolled up his sleeves with me, and among selling and customer service, he'd help with production, write invoices by hand, and pick and ship orders. I've never been above pulling and packing an order myself.

We were growing, and after running production with Barry until it was no longer sustainable with everything else we were doing, I hired Matt, a good-looking guy in his late twenties who always wore a denim jacket. He kept his head down and made it happen. Shipping a quality product on time that fit properly was the name of the game.

Shortly after, I hired Antonio, who stayed with me for the next twenty years. He was a stock boy at the FIT Library when he came to me. He was always the glue,

137

though I've never told him that. Every company needs an Antonio.

He manned the small warehouse, shipping orders and receiving all incoming packages, including fabrics, trims, etc. He ran between factories, picking up and dropping off. He helped set up trade shows and ran my personal errands. He never displayed an attitude in all those years. He got in, got it done, and got out. Consummate professional.

Next, I would hire my first assistant designer, Lynette. And along came Larry from LA, who saw how we were running the company and connected us with his former employer Carl, who sold us our ERP system that finally automated our processes. No more hand-writing invoices and the like. A new day had dawned for us.

It takes a village to succeed and the keen ability to identify emerging trends and innovate along the way. I always lived with the visual of Indiana Jones in *Raiders of the Lost Ark* blazing through the tunnel with that huge boulder rushing after him. That's kind of how I felt... all the time. If I slowed down, we'd be crushed. Fashion really is a fast-moving industry, and the more success I had, the more worried I became because I knew we had to top the numbers from the year before.

While you may have hero items that can sell one season to the next, the trends move fast. We were designing clothes nine months in advance of people wearing them. Newness needs to always be emerging so your brand looks fresh and relevant. It's clearly an industry that demands a high level of drive and initiative and one that's not suited for those content with mediocrity.

But, it's not just about looking ahead all of the time. Opportunity happens right under your nose, too, which is why it's important to have a feel for the things that are retailing in real time and to get creative and find ways to maximize the business. Through the years, we'd hit on and milk certain trends.

Eventually, we landed on two signature looks that accounted for a huge part of our early success. We hit on this stretch poplin fabric and did these shrunken three-quarter sleeve shirts and cargo pants that were trending around the year 2000. Once I saw the early response to the styles and reorders started coming in fast and furious, I got busy lab dipping our own colors with the fabric mill. We soon offered twenty custom colors in these signature silhouettes. Now, that's how to maximize a trend.

We couldn't keep them in stock. We would overcut hundreds of pieces for reorders weekly. We had three styles in the shirts and two in the pants. I remember Henri Bendel, every Monday morning, reordering the pants while Neiman Marcus would reorder the shirts, not to mention the hundreds of boutiques that were selling them. We even got a magazine cover shot with Michelle Williams wearing one of the styles.

Later, we were doing these washed silk racerback tanks with a black, wide elastic combo on the back. They were available in several solid and ombre colors. We sold thousands. We also made them private label for Scoop, which was an iconic New York retailer among the first to bridge the gap between contemporary and young designer back then.

Another item I landed on was the by-product of a trip to Paris, where I ended up in this obscure designer's boutique/atelier. The details are fuzzy about how I got there, but I definitely remember the inspiration that came from it. They were creating these bespoke styles out of actual vintage kimonos and contrasting different prints. Another example of upcycling. This was something really fresh that I hadn't seen before.

I bought one halter top and, upon my return, got busy sourcing vintage kimonos, so I could reproduce the fabrics and create my own styles in these new and novel print mixes. I tweaked the halter sample I brought back, and that became a bestseller along with a drawstring pant in the coming season.

There would be many more standout items along the way, too numerous to count. Needless to say, having these new and aspirational pieces that ring the register are integral to any brand's success.

The Fashion Hunt

Being a shopper from the time I was a pre-adolescent, I continued to shop my way through my whole career. The hunt was never over, whether I was hitting stores in LA to find new brands I didn't know when I was a buyer or shopping stores to find accounts to sell or power design inspo shopping through major cities including New York, Paris, London, Antwerp, Shanghai and ports of call like Saint Tropez and Ibiza. The list goes on.

Then, there was my true love: vintage shopping. Anywhere I went, if there was a cool, intriguing market or show happening, I had to check it out. In the early days, there were bi-annual excursions to Portobello Market in London and Clignancourt in Paris, weekly trips to 26th Street Flea and quarterly trips to The Rose Bowl in Pasadena. I was always in pursuit of fashion gold, the thing that would usher in the next trend.

I saw many East Village vintage shops make the move to Brooklyn, and I'd follow them there. As the years progressed, there'd be Manhattan Vintage, Brooklyn Flea, and A Current Affair, not to mention all the local shops in all the untold towns I visited in the US.

Then, there were the shops I frequented in the Marais in Paris. I was a regular at Rayon D'or Baggage. I could always snag a huge duffel roller case for around thirty bucks to get my stash home. I highly recommend it if you find yourself in a similar bind. Then, there was London. And when the vintage dried up there, I headed to Brighton. I've covered a lot of ground.

Aside from feeding my own wardrobe, I'd pick up vintage inspo samples for silhouette and prints mainly. Though sometimes, I'd come across a fabric I'd look to develop.

Sometimes, I traveled with my team or designer friends. But, mostly, I liked to shop alone. I had honed a sixth sense over many years and could know in around ten seconds if the place held promise. After that, I could scour the store in record time, pulling out the best items. That's how I rolled.

Whether on a shopping excursion or running around day-to-day, during every waking hour, I was a human sponge, ready to absorb everything and anything that spoke to me creatively. If people only knew the origin of the pieces we made. I could have been inspired by going to Coachella, an art show, a museum exhibition, or a botanical garden. A film or TV series, street, vintage, or luxury fashion, or just the sand on a beach that forms an unusual pattern. Or even a pack of gum.

Our best-selling cerulean blue silk began as a 5 Peppermint Gum wrapper that we sent to the mill to lab dip, believe it or not. I've never entirely known why certain things captivate me, but I trust when it happens. Let's just call it a sixth sense. And that sixth sense has rarely steered me wrong.

The featured designer at Dallas Market Week
rocking an all-time fave print: star paisley

Shaping Brand DNA

always wanted to do prints after having so much success with them early on, and I adored the creation process. So, in the early 2000s, we launched the first printed capsule group that was made of monochromatic ditsy prints in silk chiffon. I remember the Fred Segal buyer at time, John, seeing us at the Coterie in New York and him saying, "You're on to something. Keep doing this."

After we started experimenting with them, the reaction was great. So, I dove in as art director, overseeing my team, and we created the most interesting, compelling prints that no one else had. That would become our unique selling proposition, aka USP.

Unaccustomed to following trends, I always let the prints I found while hunting for vintage inspire me. Later, my team and I would curate and purchase designs from the print shows in New York or go to Indigo at Premiere Vision in Paris. But, even then, we'd have to adapt the designs and tweak them in some way to Alice & Trixify them.

We were fortunate to have others recognize and value

the things we designed through the years. Celebs from Paris Hilton to Taylor Swift and Halle Berry to Sofia Vergara, along with a host of other stars, would be seen wearing Alice & Trixie prints through the years. That would set the success trajectory and DNA of the brand for the next seventeen years and what we became widely known for: exclusive signature prints in luxe fabrics, namely silk.

I always liked the juxtaposition of combining disparate patterns, aka print mixing. Some of our greatest successes would be the border prints we designed. We'd create one allover pattern and a series of borders with different complementary motifs in varying widths. Each silhouette we created in the group would have the borders specifically engineered to fit the style so they looked purposeful, unique and upscale.

Then, there were the bespoke boho patchwork prints we became known for. Those started with my love of vintage scarves that I collected. I positioned and safety-pinned several of them together and gave the crude concoction to Elliot, my fabric supplier. He, in turn, sent it to Vietnam, and fifty-two screens later, we had a gorgeous print on silk charmeuse that would blow out in every style. We did twelve, in fact.

One time, we created these geometric patterns. There were two scales of a dot pattern in different colorways and a variegated striped pattern. We designed these cummerbund tank and halter tops that marked the beginning of a huge trend we would milk. Each pattern piece was cut in a different print. These print mixes were very unusual and the silhouettes bespoke.

You can only imagine my surprise when I saw knockoffs in the window at The Gap. True story. Imitation is the sincerest form of flattery.

Riding on their success, we created even more styles with the same attached cummerbunds that tied in the back. Women loved them because they camouflaged their muffin top, a term first coined back then associated with low-rise jeans. Our biggest customer was Saks Fifth Avenue, and they always displayed them on a T-stand merchandised with Seven jeans. They became a fashion uniform, much like the ubiquitous ones we had when I was a teen growing up in the Five Towns.

Over the years, we experimented with many other fabrics, too, such as different types of cotton, embellishments, stretch wovens, novelty pant fabrics, crochets, embroideries, laces, stretchy knits, genuine leather and suede, tweeds, vegan leather, and every kind of silk imaginable. Aside from stretch poplin, which was huge for us in the beginning, and silk, of course, we had moderate success with many of the others.

Nevertheless, the prints we developed have always remained true to my heart and the DNA of Alice & Trixie. It was the place where my creativity could soar, and the sky was the limit as to what we could design. Prints have the ability to take something from ordinary to extraordinary. We were designing bespoke art that was exclusive to us and a point of distinction from other brands. Our onlyness.

I found through the years that many women are actually afraid of prints, and color, for that matter. Some told me they didn't know how to wear them and that they were most comfortable in solid, neutral tones. I will say, though, most women do appreciate a pop color, something used in a small way, or in an unexpected place like a jacket lining or pant facing.

Being color-obsessed myself, I love it in all its forms, hot pink being my favorite well before Barbiecore was ever a thing. I relish finding it in unexpected places. Color is what attracts my eye to things. Whether it's the colors that merge together in a graffiti mural in the city, a combination used on a magazine cover or a home decor scheme, my love of color is undying. For that reason, it was a vital component of A&T's core identity.

The young girls and women who flocked to the brand bought our dresses not because they wanted to fit in but because they wanted to stand out. I coined the phrase, "Our customers are about an attitude, not an age."

Our dresses made their debut at all sorts of events: weddings, engagements, romantic dinners, coming of age parties, honeymoons, yacht soirees. The list goes on. I would think of the tagline… "Alice & Trixie: For the times of your life."

Some of the same buyers I sold as a young brand got older and kind of outgrew us, while others were ride-or-die babes, always waiting to see the next collection. Real Alice & Trixie girls, as I called them, loved bold prints and color, lots of color. And we gave it to them.

Designed for Success
The New HQ

Cut to 2005, the same year Gwen Stefani topped the charts with her first solo single, Hollaback Girl. While I was moving to Soho to live in my new loft, we moved Alice & Trixie to a 7,500-square-foot space at 265 West 37th Street.

Once again, fortune came my way in the form of an amazing space at a great price, which included a full buildout, paid for by the landlord. Thanks, Marty. We had more than ample space to grow into, which is important to consider when developing a business.

The building was home to a cross section of the fashion trades, including sewing factories, patternmaking services, textile companies, trim suppliers, production houses, and a sprinkling of brands. It was buzzing with rushed people coming and going, some with patterns and markers in hand, others carrying bolts of fabric.

And if you tried leaving the building at 5 pm, good luck! You had to let a handful of elevators pass you by, as they were packed with factory workers heading home for the night. New York style, like a can of sardines. We were in the middle of the mix, and I loved it!

Our new space inhabited half of the eleventh floor and formed the shape of a large U, with my office ceremoniously perched on the corner with city views up and down 8th Avenue and sunset views to the west up 37th Street. I had finally arrived.

The floors were done in a high gloss finish over raw cement and globe pendants hung throughout the space. No fluorescents like at Mia in Montreal. Those were reserved for the sample room, warehouse area, and bookkeeping office, where high intensity was needed for pattern making, cutting and sewing, picking orders, and looking at financial docs.

I favored a communal workspace, so the departments were adjacent to one another and could interface easily in the expansive area. It housed design, production, sample room, shipping and receiving, sales and marketing, finance and leadership. I especially loved how much square footage we were able to dedicate solely to design and product development. Plenty of space for the growing team in our new studio.

Our seasonal inspo and sketches were tacked on to mobile double-sided cork boards that glided effortlessly through the space. We had rolling racks with samples, closets filled with our print development strike-offs, file cabinets filled with various fabric headers, baker's racks that housed books, magazines, and our seasonal binders with silhouettes and prints. Chunky 5-inch binders corralled pitch sheets that we sent to the mills for coloring our prints. And aside from the Pantone color library, there was another far bigger one we created over the years with color swatches in every conceivable hue under the sun.

This set-up would be heaven for any creative. Even though I knew that then, in hindsight now, I feel I didn't appreciate it enough, for I was too busy, immersed in the high-paced hustle and grind required to make it in this industry.

During the next couple of years, the operation expanded with the demands of a growing fashion brand. The design team grew to three, with at least one designer specifically working on prints. There were various assistants and always a gaggle of interns running around.

I loved being able to illuminate the path for the next generation of fashion newbies. I always felt it was my responsibility to offer a valuable experience for these rookies. After all, I was once in their shoes, and without my mentors, I could never have achieved the level of success I had.

The lessons they learned working in an operation like ours were unmatched. They got to see so many facets of the industry at play in real time. The vast majority had their sights on design, though many changed their major after being exposed to an area they had never considered before.

We had a full sample room with three patternmakers, a cutter, and five sewers, which acted as a mini factory at times. This supercharged our design and development output, and sometimes, we even did small production runs in-house when the units were low and the sample room was light on work. Our bulks, on the other hand, continued to be outsourced.

During peak times, additional cutters were brought in to assist us, like when we were getting a new season ready to go to market. With five new sample collections in development for the reps, it was chaotic, to say the least. To further supplement the in-house team, we sent samples to be cut by our bulk cutter, Mr. Ma, or sewn by our main factory owned by veteran husband and wife duo, Verna and Louie.

These times were intense when all hands were needed on deck. So, above all the noise – the rat-tat-tat of our Juki sewing machines, the buzz of our cutting blades, and the occasional sample room squabble amongst that crew – we had to stay on top of every single aspect and detail. This all required an elaborate system of sample tracking to make sure we received everything back in time for our deadlines.

What patterns are ready with the sew by sample, fabric, and any trims? Which sample yardage arrived and which are we still waiting for? Same with trims. What's cut? What's on deck to be cut? What do we have a pattern for but no fabric, yet, or fabric for but no pattern? What do we have fabric and a pattern for but no trim or combo fabric? What's being cut and sewn in-house, and what's going out for cutting and sewing? How are the live model fittings going, and what corrections still need to be made to the first patterns before we cut them again? Where are all of the finished garments, and when are they scheduled to arrive?

It really takes a village to bring a brand to life. With each new collection having around 120 pieces, on average, all these moving parts were a lot to manage.

Much like a symphony, all things must move together in unison toward a common goal to create harmony.

Sounds like nirvana, right? I assure you it's not. There is no perfection, and there are always bumps along the way. But, we pressed on to do better each day. Someone wise once told me that there will always be waves, you just need to learn how to ride the surf.

We weren't sending a rocket to the moon, after all. We'd have to remind ourselves of that fact on the daily, if we were to keep our sanity. Things could really spin out of control otherwise, especially if we let ourselves lead with emotion, which I often found myself doing. Take a deep breath and carry on. It's only fashion. Easy to say that now.

To keep up with the increasing demands, the team continued to grow. During our highest volume periods, we had two bookkeepers, one for accounts receivable and one for accounts payable. When dealing with chains and department stores, they usually took advantage and tried to charge back dollars for various reasons, such as not labeling boxes correctly or shipping on the wrong hangers. Even the boutiques would try to deduct for any reason. So, it was critical to keep a watchful eye on incoming funds to make sure they weren't taking wrongful deductions.

Our domestic sales functions were outsourced to regional multi-line showrooms in the South, West, and Northeast. This allowed us to focus solely on design and manufacturing, though eventually, we brought the Northeast back in-house, with a team of three at the height. We outsourced PR intermittently, as well.

As the years progressed and we became more rooted

in our HQ, I continued to embrace the role of creative director, overseeing all design, photography, and content creation while continuing to act as CEO. I had a full plate, and there was never a dull moment. But, thriving on the adrenaline, I couldn't have imagined it any other way.

The Design Process
A Coveted Look

A fashion brand is unique in that we are always changing with the seasons, creating newness. As such, we don't create and perfect one product, then set it and forget it, like many other businesses do. It's particularly grueling to be consistently reinventing the wheel.

So, from the outside, it probably looked like utter chaos. And believe me, it was sometimes. But, I assure you, there was a method to the madness.

We designed five seasonal collections a year: fall, holiday, resort, spring, and summer. It was usually twelve or so weeks from concept to finished collection. The beginning of the season started with determining the design direction.

Let's take spring as an example. That was one of our most important seasons. We'd start with the print development because it was our signature DNA and took the most time to develop, execute and receive our sample yardage.

We didn't usually follow what the trend reports were forecasting. My method was to shop for prints and let them speak to me. It was much more intuitive than blindly following what the trend houses were projecting.

Once we did all of our digging and research to find the best prints, we'd have a meeting, kind of like the buying meetings I'd had at Mia. Instead of an oval conference table, we'd sit on the comfy sunken leather couch and stare at all the prints hanging on the show bars. Then, some of us would get up and move them around in an effort to coordinate and merchandise them.

We'd hold them up to our bodies and critique them one by one. It's important not to have competing designs that can cannibalize one another. They can split sales and confuse the buyer which is a universal no-no in commerce. An uncertain buyer typically doesn't buy.

Varying scale was important, too. The prints needed to stand on their own but flow together like different verses in the same song. Going back and forth to the printer, we'd zoom in and out, playing with scale, and hang the printouts on the show bars with the other designs. We'd sit and stare some more.

Once we made our selections, we needed to get the prints ready to go to the mill for strike-offs. This is where the real heavy lifting happened and the art direction came in.

If the print was purchased from a design studio, they gave us a digital file along with the fabric printed artwork. We invariably had changes we wanted to make, so I had to communicate that to the print designer. If we purchased vintage, the garment needed to be scanned in and the file cleaned, which took a while. Other times, we started from scratch, piecing together different motifs. This process took the longest time with the exploration of many renderings.

Often, throughout the process, we'd make these large scale printouts and hold them up to our body, creasing the paper to look like shirred fabric. This helped us isolate any motif and layout flaws and areas that needed overall improvement.

Once we settled on the designs, and while the files were being made mill ready, we tackled the coloring of the prints. This was one of my favorite parts of the process. Aside from my team's efforts, I got to sit on my computer and work in Photoshop, immersing myself in the fantasy of color for several hours at a time. I felt like I was a kid using crayons in a coloring book.

After developing a gajillion color combos, we'd isolate the ones we liked best. Then, it was time to assign the actual color standards we'd send to the mill, placing them on pitch sheets. We were prone to over-develop, sometimes submitting as many as ten colorways for a print, when we only needed two or three to make it on to the line.

We liked to hedge our bets because it wasn't an exact science, and we wanted to make sure we'd have enough of a choice when the strike offs came in. As such, this part was an elaborate process that could take more than a day, with all hands on deck, finding the exact colors in our extraordinarily large color library. While many designers, if not most, stick solely to the Pantone Color System, we didn't, which is why our color combos were as bespoke as the prints we developed.

Simultaneously, there was usually one designer exploring and researching silhouette ideas and shopping for any trims. The seasonal styles we eventually developed were a fusion of my vintage finds reimagined, inspo pictures from my shopping trips, previous bestsellers that were still relevant, and new styles designed in-house, some inspired by what the heritage luxury designers were sending down the runway.

We created a line plan that covered all the shapes we felt were important, first determining any best-sellers to carry forward from the previous season. Then, after many sketch reviews, we started to plug in the new styles we'd chosen for the upcoming season. These were then given to our patternmakers to create the first patterns that we would cut, sew and fit in similar fabrics we had on hand.

About three weeks after submitting the prints, we received our first strike-offs. The anticipation was palpable as we unfolded the fabric cuts that were usually around a quarter of a yard. Passing them back and forth between us, we'd drape them against our bodies and then walk over to one of our full-length mirrors and admire, ascertain any flaws that needed correcting, or simply cast aside the ones we didn't like at all.

Sometimes, we were disappointed to find that the mill didn't follow our color standards or they made a mistake on the actual print registration. The thought that you have to crack a few eggs to make an omelet comes to mind here. Shit happens, and it's not an exact science.

In contrast, we were psyched much of the time with prints and colorways coming out better than we could have imagined. Once we addressed any concerns and approved the strike-offs we selected, it took another two weeks to receive our sample yardage.

In a perfect world, the sample yardage arrived, and all first patterns were corrected and ready to be cut. Not to disappoint, but this rarely happens, unless maybe you take six months or more to develop a collection. In fashion, though, with everything moving fast, we never had that luxury of time.

Plus, even if everything was ready, there would be a bottleneck at the cutting stage. So, that's how we found ourselves having to micromanage every step to get the collection in on time. It's a very delicate balance to coordinate so many moving parts. But, we made it without fail every time.

With the demanding deadlines that are a hallmark of our industry, one has to adopt an attitude of, We get it done, no matter what. The wheels are always in motion. No letting up on the pedal, ever, and so it goes.

Above: Having fun making huge doggie bags for NYC subway riders. Long story.

Right: Arriving to work at HQ. Pumped to start the day.

Spring shoot in Connecticut. Loved how the colors popped in this exaggerated mosaic print.

Summer shoot in the Hamptons during the golden hour. One of my fave styles ever.

The Photoshoots
Behind the Scenes

hile we were winding down the sampling process for the newest collection, we turned our attention toward coordinating the photo shoots. There would be two, in fact.

In one day, we'd shoot upwards of 120 looks, all product shots for our line sheets and a select few for e-comm. As the years went by and technology improved with digital, the store buyers expected more, and hand-sketched line- sheets gave way to live model photos, as a necessity to get orders.

On the next day, we were on location doing lifestyle photos for lookbooks and the website. This was a highly auspicious day with the seasonal vision finally brought to life through imagery. It was beyond thrilling to see the collection sing as the models moved. Even though we designed everything and knew the styles intimately, they came to life on the body, and it was like love at first sight.

We coordinated photoshoots five times a year with each new collection. For each one, along with the models, we needed to book a photographer and hair and makeup people, which were typically found through agencies. We'd review their digital portfolios to make our choices. Each creative was scrutinized based on different criteria.

On the photographers, I looked at lighting and overall style of the shots. On the hair and makeup, I was looking for how they elevated more natural looks as opposed to flashy, avant-garde, editorial makeup and hair because that wasn't the brief for us.

We'd have a model casting next. We'd go through the various agency websites to see the digital books, choose the models we liked best and have them come to our HQ for a go-see. They inevitably sent other girls that we didn't request on top, usually newer girls. It gave them more experience and the possibility of getting booked. It kind of annoyed us, though, since it was a waste of our time, and we felt bad briskly sending them off.

It was very important to have each model try on a variety of our silhouettes, so we could see how they looked on their body type. We also didn't want them to be much smaller than our sample size so the clipping would be minimal the day of the shoot. Time is money, and the longer it took to make the clothes look presentable, the more we risked moving into costly overtime.

We were mindful of how their legs looked in short dresses and how their shoulders looked in cami, strapless, and halter styles. We wanted to see them in pants to check for length issues and overall fit. We usually looked to book models that were around 5'10". We thought they wore the clothes the best.

Next, we requested them to pose for some shots. This

part I found mission critical because if the model didn't know how to change facial expression or move freely, showing a variety of flattering poses, it became a nightmare on the day of the shoot.

We also examined their hair texture. Some models have fine hair that won't hold a wave or curl. So, if that's the look you want, it will be hard to realize the day of the shoot, even with the best hair stylist, unless they are using extensions, which takes more time and effort. Their complexion was scrutinized, too, because if they have any type of obvious skin condition, it can be hard to mask with makeup.

Once we assembled a dream team, we looked to work together on subsequent shoots. It made the shoot so much less stressful when all the quantities were known. We even used models for a few seasons. When the synergy works and the creativity flows, it's an enjoyable day, and the shots come out great. That's why in Hollywood, too, you'll often see a group of creatives working together over and over again.

We spent a few days, at least, getting ready for the shoots. We created a swipe file for hair and makeup, poses and lighting. We decided the look and feel of the shoot we wanted and set out to procure the missing elements. We'd pick up any footwear, accessories, and jewelry and shop for any necessary props, if needed. Then, we'd have a meeting to style all the looks. This is where we began to see our design vision come to life.

Acting as art director, I'd scout for places that would give us the widest variety of backgrounds for the shots. Over the years, we shot at photo studios with a wide assortment of props, private lofts (my own included), and homes that had interesting architecture and furnishings. We shot in the Hamptons on more than one occasion, Rockaway Beach, Catalina Beach Club, downtown Brooklyn in Dumbo, and the streets of NYC.

But, once the shoots wrapped, the party wasn't over, it was just beginning. We'd have to isolate and choose the best photos, which involved sifting through thousands of images. This was one of my favorite times. After all the pandemonium we endured for weeks, I finally got to settle into my comfy Aeron chair for hours going through the images.

But, the respite was brief because we were on our way next to the seasonal trade shows and regional market weeks to sell the collection to our stores. And remember, this was all happening while we were neck-deep in production fittings, pattern corrections, and cutting and sewing for the current season that was about to ship. All this in the city that never sleeps. Nor did we!

The Tides of Change

While we were busy staking our claim as a respected NYC fashion brand, the garment district continued to see heavy change. The mass exodus that began in the '90s continued into the aughts. I remember one-by-one at an increasingly rapid pace, the industry was losing its manufacturing players.

Due to its cheap labor, China provided lower prices that companies couldn't resist. So, production started moving there mostly and to other countries. Everywhere but the US.

I remember the initial shock I felt hearing about NY designers that were practically household names leaving the city to produce overseas. Only now, they started moving their sample rooms there, too, leaving domestic factory owners scrambling again to find more work to survive. Factories rolled up and closed or left the city due to the rising costs of operating there.

Consolidations started happening, too. There used to

be around thirty button companies to choose from when I started A&T in '97. By 2007, there were probably around seven. Some joined forces while others just went out of business.

There was further fragmentation as the once showroom-heavy garment district began to disperse, with sales reps and brands moving to places like Soho and the Meatpacking District. In the aftermath, the once fully-occupied skyscrapers all along Broadway and Seventh Avenue and even some on the side streets, like W 39th and W 40th, saw lots of vacancies.

I saw the exciting, dynamic industry that I loved and grew up in slowly vanish before my eyes. I still find it disheartening to think about. Tech companies started rolling in, and today, it's a potpourri of every kind of business you could imagine, from escape rooms to acting studios, event spaces to architectural firms and plenty of not-so-sexy businesses in between. Hotels sit where the outdoor parking lots were, and commercial buildings converted to residential apartments round out the rest.

As I witnessed this evolution happening in real time, I couldn't even think of what outsourcing my manufacturing would mean. Having my own mini factory in my design studio was a luxury I wasn't willing to part with. It cost more to maintain through the years, but as long as we were in the black, I didn't care. And we were, so the sample room stayed. Now, if I had a CFO, I'm sure they would have seen things differently and tried to convince me otherwise. I did it my way, though, the way I knew worked.

Made in New York or Bust

Overseas production just wasn't my jam. I had a deep fear of it, in fact. Reminds me of the irrational thought of mistakenly cutting two left legs that worried me at the beginning. I could never consider moving my production unless I saw the factories with my own eyes, and even then I had hesitation because I loved being so hands-on. I liked to see all my babies go from initial concept to final creation and all the stages in between.

It was exhilarating having the ability to react when it came to a new trend I felt was emerging. I could execute fast. If the fabric was in-house, one day was all it took to make a pattern and sample usually. It was easy to experiment with my every whim. A designer's ultimate bliss.

It was also super convenient to have things close. Our marking and grading service, Accurate Patterns, was a block over on W 38th St., and we were sewing in factories within blocks and later in Brooklyn. Once the fabric hit, as long as our production patterns were done, we were ready to roll. As a result, we were able to turn goods superfast in two weeks comfortably, or even less if we needed to make a tight delivery deadline. That would never be the case with China.

In addition, because their production lead times took much longer on average, orders needed to be placed far in advance. This meant brands would have to place their buys with the factories ahead of getting all the buyer's orders in hand. This is risky and the reason why you see name brands in stores like TJ Maxx and online retailer Gilt Group.

I call these store buys "safety net orders." These retailers buy upfront and know they will be shipped approximately ninety days after the full price stores get the merch. This has given way to sixty and even thirty days out. These orders were mandatory for brands to get because it also helped them meet the large minimums China had for years.

These big orders can also become the life blood of scaling businesses since they allow for shipping more product, in turn driving growth. Plus, brands need these relationships so they can dump goods that may be returned from big accounts, like department stores.

Maybe there's a production error that leaves an overcut or a quality or fit issue, and the goods need a place to disappear. It's a tricky balance, though, because a brand, a new brand especially, risks dilution. The brand must always be protected.

In retrospect, with cut-to-order domestic, we were acting more sustainably with regard to waste than many brands out there. We could purchase the fabric ahead of time, collect the orders, and try to bump it up if they started to exceed the initial buy. That way, we'd go off sale once the fabric was done and cut to order, planning to have no excess. We used to plan overcuts on key items in the old days. But, as time went on, we rarely overcut anything because the stores reordered less and less, even if they sold out.

An additional perk of having close access to our cutting room, where we did our bulks, was that we could see with our own eyes if there was potential fabric waste once the marker was laid out on the table. The marker is a template of all the pattern pieces. Depending on how they lock in with one another, there are typically parts of the spread fabric that don't get cut into.

As a result, there will be these large wads of fabric just dumped in the trash bin along the way. In our case, we created patterns for buyer giveaways like eye masks and cosmetic cases so we could use the otherwise wasted fabric. It was our little way to act sustainably while showing our appreciation to the buyers.

But, the best-laid plans, as they say, because for some reason, we invariably had extra merch floating around. Whether it was a canceled order, merchandise a store returned for exchange, or in rare cases, a small production mistake, there was always something hanging in the warehouse.

In the messy, chaotic world of fashion manufacturing, where Murphy's law prevails each day, anything that can go wrong will go wrong. I learned to put out the fires first and ask questions later. It's just the nature of the beast.

But, I was in the game, following every move in real time. Making things overseas felt like a remote spectator sport, where you have little control over the outcomes. I'd rather be on the field in the stadium any day.

Ultimately, I clung to my old school ways of staying domestic, which undeniably had its advantages. Not only were we benefiting from the fast turnarounds and running more sustainably, I relished being in the frenzy of things and the creative freedom that it afforded me. New York made, we were in heart of it all, and I loved it!

Navigating a Recession with Grace & Business Acumen

2007 was a banner year for us and for Justin Timberlake, who had seven songs on the charts. Alice & Trixie had been increasing sales year-over-year since 1997. Orders kept coming at a rapid speed, and our HQ was in utter mayhem, trying to keep up.

I'd walk by desks with stacks of orders waiting to be entered manually into our system. We were ordering more and more fabric and upping the size of our cutting tickets. With Saks Fifth Avenue alone, we did a million and a half dollars that year. We were unstoppable, or so I thought.

Then, in 2008, at the pinnacle of our growth and Katy Perry's, too, with her breakout single "I Kissed a Girl," the Great Recession hit, and its huge economic meltdown leveled the playing field. Back then, I would say we had all been living in a bubble on cruise control, with not a cloud on the horizon. And then, we suddenly hit turbulence and needed to get back to the controls. Things got serious real fast.

It was survival of the fittest. The trees were shaking,

and all the low-hanging fruit suddenly dropped. It kind of went like this...

Stores that had been around for a long time with owners who were nearing retirement decided it was time to close shop. Others, who thought all they needed was a love of fashion but had no idea how to run a business, shuttered not by choice. These were a vast majority of boutique owners, which consisted of two subsets.

One included the wives and girlfriends of hedge fund guys and pro athletes, whose significant other bankrolled the whole thing, and it was more of a vanity project. The other was made up of owners who were more serious and had invested their own hard-earned money or that of friends and family. In either case, they possessed little to no viable business skills, certainly none that would support them in getting through a severe economic downturn successfully.

The ones left standing were the veteran retailers and others, those with strong entrepreneurial expertise. Though, even they canceled orders and tightened their belts... for good. I never again saw big orders like we used to get from the boutiques. They were even hesitant to place reorders on things that blew out. Many were relieved that the product sold out in the first place and were content to just move on. They proceeded with caution for years to come.

Cut the expenses, but don't slash your prices. Players who lacked foresight made the mistake of blindly lowering prices, and they never recouped. There were fewer stores to sell to, and the ones left bought frugally. With the cost of goods to manufacture not going down, profit margins were slimmer, incoming sales lower, and they devalued their brands in the process. All in all, a recipe for disaster.

The retailers did this, too. Some started carrying cheap product, but they just hurt their store's image and made less money in the long run because customers didn't buy more as a result of the lower prices.

We were very intentional during this time not to hurt the brand. We lowered prices roughly fifteen percent, not too crazy, showing sensitivity and awareness of the climate, and we found other ways to bring value to the stores.

I had an idea to create a capsule group and call it Best Bets after a long running column in New York Magazine. I knew we had to offer sharper price points. But, taking the things we already made and just chopping the price is just bad business.

I looked at our overall costing and fabric consumptions. It was clear that the fabric accounted for a big part of the pricing. If I could create styles that used less of the expensive fabric and combo that with a lower-priced fabric, it would be a meaningful reduction to start. And so I did.

We used a lycra knit that was form-fitting on the bodice paired with silk bottom panels and created design variations on the theme. Labor costs also came down because they had a simpler construction with fewer details. They sold like hotcakes.

I also launched a lower-priced label named Maiya to pick up the slack in sales, but it was just a temporary band-aid to get through. Over the years, I launched other brands in tandem with Alice & Trixie if I saw a void in the market. There was Ritual, George, and November Four. But, they were usually short-lived when I realized that, without their own teams, running them just divided our attention.

We even did menswear under the label Ralph & Norton, the husbands of Alice & Trixie. Saks retailed and reordered the slim fit printed shirts we made. Though, building one brand is hard enough, let alone two or more without dedicated staff.

One that I thought held the most promise was called Jack. We made menswear-inspired trousers and shorts in a variety of European stretch woven novelty fabrics. Obviously, I had gotten over my irrational fear by then. LOL. We were already in the seventh year of a denim cycle that historically lasts as long. So, I thought the market would be ripe for something new. We did marginally well at the time, but denim just stayed queen and still hasn't gone away, even to this day.

In the end, by applying all the knowledge and wisdom I'd gained over the years, along with boundless creativity and a bit of good fortune, we made it through the Great Recession. Onward and upward, it was time to thrive again.

Back in the Game

usiness was back on an upward swing after a couple of rough years. We made it through. But, we took some hits.

We lost our biggest account, Saks Fifth Avenue after two years of declining volume from them. They found opportunities with newer brands that were far less expensive but offered similar product to what we were doing. They were also chasing the younger Barneys customer, who they saw as edgier than A&T by that point. The irony was not lost on me that they filled the gap with a new startup brand co-founded by a former employee. Fashion is a competitive beast, and you're never safe.

Since they were just starting out, they didn't have the overhead of a larger brand like ours, so their pricing could be more competitive. They also made everything in China and India. One playbook is to come into the market at a lower price point to gain market share and then inch prices up seasonally. That's what this brand did. So, in just a few years, their prices were comparable with ours.

Soon, though, we were approached by a European distributor out of Belgium. Because our brand had been selling so well for some of their retailers that had been buying direct from us, they sought us out. We joined forces with them and learned that their customer was a designer store who looked to Alice & Trixie as a lower price point for their affluent clientele. Very different product positioning than the US, where we were considered the high-end price point in many of our stores.

This joint venture helped to boost our sales and offset any domestic losses in our business. I attended the trade shows in Paris, Milan, London, and Berlin, where they showcased the collection. The reception and enthusiasm for the line was invigorating. Things were looking up again.

E-Commerce
& Social Media Rising

We had just turned the corner into the 2010s, and I knew the world was changing fast with the way social media and the internet was evolving. I remember going to a conference in New York, where breakout YouTube star Casey Neistat and Warby Parker's Dave Gilboa were participants in the panel discussions that day. I had a deep intuition that fashion e-commerce at scale would be fast on its heels. And it was.

Before the terms social media and bloggers entered our cultural vernacular, the brands, retailers, and fashion magazines were the only ones that had the ability to influence style. Eventually, celebrities would be added to the list, who were featured mainly in the weeklies. It was pretty much guaranteed that if a celeb was wearing your brand in Us Weekly or a similar mag, the style would sell out.

Then, the nascent blog sphere rose up in the wake of twelve year-old Tavi Gevinson rising to fame. With the internet and social media bringing about the democratization of fashion, the space became overcrowded with many voices and retail distribution channels, with online being the biggest disruptor.

Being a wholesale brand, there were many internal discussions about how we could create an online presence for ourselves without pissing off and ultimately losing our loyal retail brick and mortar customers. Though, it remained just that, a discussion. Little did we know then that elevating online brand awareness would help everyone in the long run.

Cut to 2013. Lorde's anti-pop pop single, "Royals," peaked at number one for nine weeks. And Alice & Trixie peaked, too, with its second record-breaking year. It was so stellar, in fact, that it culminated in the million-dollar bonus I took at the behest of my accountant. We were back.

Eventually, we were approached by someone who was doing e-comm for other wholesale brands. One of my friends was already working with him, so we thought we'd give it a try. He was a gateway solution.

We were novices, knowing nothing about how to run an e-comm site. So, we outsourced it to him, giving him 30% of the revenue generated and got our feet wet. He was responsible for shooting the product on models and uploading the photos onto the website his team created. We, in turn, shipped him the merch in bulk, and he fulfilled the orders to the customers. Easy peasy, for us.

Only thing was that we were so busy with our booming wholesale business that the site was an afterthought. We didn't put much effort or care into what we were sending him at first, just stuff we had left over. Eventually, we did buys specifically allocated for the site. Though, in the end, selling onesies over our bulk shipments to our retailers still seemed a bit of a pain in the ass. I also found it hard to really milk online sales because if we had an even spread of styles and sizes and sold out of the winners, that was it.

We could have sold tons more while the other less favorable styles just sat. There's that 80/20 rule. But, no one had a crystal ball or the confidence to go that deep into any one style without it first being a proven bestseller. So, this severely limited the ability to maximize sales.

After a couple years of half-assing it, we sat at the Soho House with Adam, the e-comm guy, and he pushed us to get serious. He knew the opportunity that we still needed to be sold on. It was really about bandwidth at the time and knowing where our bread was being buttered.

Ironically, once we started to get serious, we found fault with Adam's performance in how our website looked and with the off-brand models he was using. I guess Maryland isn't the model capital of the world. Suffice to say, once it got my full attention around 2015, a new day had dawned.

With our competitors popping up everywhere, with their own brick and mortar shops and e-commerce sites, the retail stores seemed less likely to drop us. The tides had turned. The same people who would complain through the years that we were selling another store too close to them had to just buckle up and take the ride. Business had changed forever.

With a new logo and custom designed site that took months, we launched our own Shopify store and got an in-house person to run it. We connected with an agency that was helping other wholesale brands that were doing paid performance marketing. Think Facebook ads, Google ad words, etc.

We were like babies learning to walk. We didn't know the questions to ask or what things meant. Acronyms like CAC, CLT, AOV, ROAS. Terms like customer journey, and welcome email series were all new to me. But, I dug in alongside my team to learn the ways of the new world.

To command in business is to be a life-long learner. Smart people ask questions to get the answers they need to excel. I was keen to understand everything and welcomed all the learning, though having to recalibrate after being so self-assured for so long was humbling. Looking back, connecting the dots seems easy now. But, at the time, all this info was mind-boggling.

The Big Sourcing Trip

t's now 2015. Among dramatic headlines of the Paris terror attacks and Caitlyn Jenner coming out, Adele released, hit single "Hello." And I finally made the big sourcing trip, saying hello to China and Hong Kong with the notion that maybe we would move some of our production there.

My assistant, Chanthan, and I made the trip together. She had been to Asia multiple times when she worked for another brand. So, she was my wing girl and guide at times.

The first stop was Guangzhou for the Canton Fair, a bi-annual import and export trade fair, where they feature international consumer goods. It's the oldest and largest of its kind. Ginormous in size is an understatement, if you can imagine, and fashion products are only one segment of the show. There, we were exposed to a wide variety of suppliers that manufactured garments, accessories and shoes. Yes, and leather shoes, the category that, years ago, I never could have imagined being made in China.

To my surprise, I saw one of our exclusive prints in a booth. Having purchased that print from a textile design studio out of London, I'm not sure if the studio was selling the same design to others, which is suspect and not a reputable business practice, or they knocked it off from our line. Either way, I wasn't happy.

But, nothing shocks me in this business. People are getting knocked off all the time. Nothing is ever sacred. One time, I remember Karl Lagerfeld being asked how he felt about his designs being copied. He replied that he'd start worrying when they stopped. It's the curse of the relevant, I'd say.

I took the unspoken compliment, and after exploring the show for two days and meeting with several suppliers there, we were ready for our next adventure, the Guangzhou fashion district. This place was like New York in the '80s but on steroids, and lots of them. I had never before seen a place that buzzed more than New York.

The whole scene was invigorating. Fiercely determined motorists careened through the streets on these cycle rickshaws piled high with bolts of fabric honking their horns for pedestrians to get out of the way. It was utter mayhem, and I loved it!

We ducked out of the chaos and into this big building with a huge atrium that had showrooms carrying every type of fabric under the sun. Huge display cases lined the ultra-wide corridors and housed fabric samples and swatch cards that were ours for the taking. I mean, unreal.

Some had a plethora of beautiful colors that I'd end up using as color standards for some of our best prints. We made our way to a balcony, where I took lots of video to document the bedlam happening below in the streets. I thought, Only seeing is believing.

Afterwards, at the risk of being run over, we dodged and weaved our way through the traffic to the other side of the street and entered their trim marketplace. Another frenetic environment, there was a maze of bustling narrow corridors that housed small booths, where I saw families sitting together, setting rhinestones one by one to create highly embellished trims. Handmade is really handmade. It was all so fascinating and surreal.

After this unforgettable, whirlwind experience in Guangzhou, we flew to Shenzhen, where we'd meet with a factory that we had actually done business with on a couple of private label programs for Neiman Marcus Last Call as a test. The factory had a driver waiting to collect us from the airport and swiftly took us there.

Upon our arrival, after pleasantries and introductions, the business development team whisked us away to a nearby restaurant for lunch. It was there that the kind of young, fortyish factory owner joined us, arriving in a different car with her driver. She had a cosmopolitan style and spoke perfect English, which was a stark contrast to the factory owners I knew in New York who seemed less worldly with many barely speaking the language.

We were ushered into a building, seemingly in the middle of nowhere, past live fish in tanks and chefs graciously waiting behind a counter. We walked by decorative plates of fresh greens and were brought through a fancy hallway with closed doors at intervals. They cordially escorted us into one of the private rooms, where we took our seats at a big, round table.

The meal began immediately. There were hot plates with stews and different types of noodles and fresh shellfish on beds of ice. Then, they brought a stream of delicacies I've never seen or tasted before.

Our conversation was casual and light with some laughter thrown in. Reminded me of the days when they used to feed us buyers in the showrooms. With our satisfied bellies, we went back to the factory. Then, it was all business as they proceeded to give us a full tour of their operation.

Back at their main campus, they developed a variety of other fabrics, and it was exhilarating to see them weaving, dying and printing all the different textiles in this vast facility. I had only seen something even remotely like this once before at a printing plant in North Carolina I visited back in the '90s when I was repping NC Love. But, this experience blew that away. This mill was doing record high volume, and they were also supplying the fabrics to other manufacturers.

The cutting and sewing areas were vast, some not operating to their full capacity, housing additional sewing machines with no operators and cutting tables with no fabric being spread. They had large spaces devoted to patternmaking and marking and grading. We were made privy to the production of some other well-known brands in the end stages of the manufacturing process. Some things were being pressed and others were being cleaned of extra threads, while completely finished garments at the final stage were being hung and poly-bagged.

I wasn't entirely sure if it was a myth from the Far East,

but I had always heard that workers lived at the factories. I can now confirm this to be true since I saw it with my own two eyes. The buildings they inhabited were a mere stone's throw from the factory. They stayed in these quarters for long periods of time, only leaving to visit family intermittently and on holidays like Chinese New Year, which lasts for a couple of weeks, give or take. It really was a different world, where productivity reigned as the factory's absolute top priority.

Theirs was a completely vertical operation, which means not only did they cut and sew the garments, but they produced the fabric, as well. In the case of silk, which we used mainly, it's spun and woven from filaments harvested from the boiled cocoons of the silkworm. They had a silkworm farm located nearby which was incredible to see. We peaked into a building that had these round bamboo trays where the silkworms were fed their mulberry leaves.

Silk's rich history began in China, and this factory played a significant role in its heritage. A short drive from their factory, sat their very own museum. We were taken there and had the opportunity to learn about the origin and early manufacturing of the textile, step-by-step.

The exhibit characterized how this was done through the decades, beginning with their use of elaborate, manual, wooden apparatuses, the first looms used to weave the silk fibers into actual fabric. Further on, they displayed extravagant garments embellished with exquisite embroidery. This was an unexpected part of our time there but incredibly memorable amidst an already wondrous adventure.

I wore this t-shirt to death. It defined me.

The Verdict

O ur visit to the factory in Shenzhen was fascinating with memories that will last a lifetime. And after all the touring and discussion about our potential to do future business together, they bid us farewell with some tips for our next stop, Shanghai. One of which was Green Massage, which I highly recommend, should you find yourself there.

Arriving in Shanghai felt like a respite from all the stimulation thrust upon us since we had gotten to China. Taking it a bit easier, it felt more vacation-like. We shopped the retail stores one day and visited a huge, traditional marketplace the next, ending our day at The Bund, where we had gorgeous, unobstructed views of their modern skyline. Shanghai was very cool. Certain areas reminded me of the nicer parts of LA, and I loved it.

While walking around there, I was solicited by a man selling retractable selfie sticks. It was funny because I had just seen one for the first time being used by a girl at an outdoor cafe where we had breakfast. I shooed him away, but he kept lowering the price as he walked alongside me, and I would become the proud owner of a selfie stick for the equivalent of about three bucks. LOL.

After a relaxing, bespoke massage, we said goodbye to Shanghai and made our way to Hong Kong. There, it was super cool and had a cosmopolitan feel with beautiful, mountainous vistas. The city is so hilly in parts that next to the steep staircases, they had escalator-like monorails to take you up and down to certain streets.

The majestic peaks were a serene backdrop to the vibrant metropolis with the velocity of New York's Times Square but on every corner. The only word that truly fits is pandemonium. That place made New York feel slightly sleepy, if you can imagine.

It struck me funny that there were several malls, all nearby one another. And there was a mania among the shoppers that we lacked in America. While our real estate developers were thinking about how to repurpose vacant storefronts and reimagine the mall experience, Hong Kong's physical shopping was alive and well.

We visited a couple more factories right outside of Hong Kong but none as big and exciting as the Shenzhen factory. They looked rather similar to the ones we had in New York.

But in the end, after all the razzle-dazzle, I had a decision to make. Did I want to leave all I'd ever known and move our production to this faraway place with its new rules, or stay in familiar, local surroundings, where I knew the whole system by heart?

By this time, China prices had risen, and I didn't feel the moderate savings were worth the tradeoff of losing total control. Plus, if there were certain order minimums, we could potentially be stuck with extra inventory. This would eat into the bottom line even further, closing the gap on any savings.

When starting with any new factory there is an incubation period to see if you can work well together over the long haul. Is communication timely and flowing easily? Are they fully comprehending your comments on aspects of the production run?

When none of this is face-to-face or transmitted verbally, it takes more effort to get your point across. The language barrier is often an issue, and many times, this leads to mistakes. I know many designers whose initial excitement quickly turned to frustration and dismay when they had to sacrifice their original design due to poor communication and execution on the part of the factory.

Though, I was told time and again by my US reps that if we could get our prices down we'd do more volume. And moving production overseas would have helped us accomplish that. But, there would have been sacrifices in the long run.

Often, as volume grows with larger retailers, profit margins thin out considerably, and your brand risks overexposure with the possibility of being sold at lower prices than your suggested retails. This creates a loss of exclusivity and dilutes its perceived value in the marketplace. For these reasons, I was fiercely obsessed with protecting the integrity and quality of the brand and the loyal retailers I was selling by not blowing up the distribution.

But, most importantly, my margins were always healthy, and I liked it that way and so did my accountant. More volume doesn't always equate to more money on the bottom line. And bigger orders mean bigger problems. Doing a healthy multi-million dollar business annually compensated me well with fewer headaches.

Now, had I had a partner who encouraged me, it might have been a different story. On my own, I was risk averse, though, and truth be told that choked the business' growth. In hindsight, although it's what I wanted, consciously choosing to stay domestic hurt us. I slept well at night, but we had an invisible ceiling on our success.

I saw other brands exploding around me. But, in those cases, there were usually partnerships composed of a creative lead who oversaw design and front-facing activities alongside a COO who executed to bring the vision to life. To me, those are the best business marriages. But, I wasn't in one of those.

All things considered, aside from those couple of private label programs we did there for Neiman Marcus to increase our thin margins, I made the executive decision not to move any of our branded production overseas.

Too Little Too Late

fter the high point of 2013 and seeing some other brands being acquired and rolled up into bigger companies, thoughts of selling A&T began to seep in. Mind you, for a long time, it never occurred to me that I was building a valuable asset. For as savvy and street smart as I was, this eluded me.

Subconsciously, I was in this industry for the long haul, something woven into the fabric of my being since I was a kid. I never started A&T with some grand plan to build it up and sell it. This was my livelihood. There was no formal exit strategy in place. Death, maybe? LOL

Therefore, I had no idea how to embark on a transaction of that magnitude. I was especially perplexed by how valuations were determined. How much could I even get if I exited? I've always hated numbers. I even had to go to summer school for Algebra in 7th grade.

I recall proposing to my accountant, Larry, the idea of selling. He quickly retorted in his gruff Long Island accent, "How can you sell the business? You are the business." This gave me pause at first.

He was right, though. The business could not run on its own without me. While it's important to be the driving force as a founder, you can't be the only force. It's critical to empower others in your organization, and I hadn't entirely done that.

Undeterred, though, I continued to dig deeper and learned that selling a business is much like selling a house. Houses sell for the highest value when they need no repair. Homes that need a new roof, for instance, sell at a discounted price. So, I had to examine my business and isolate any flaws or areas that required improvement, so I could, in turn, procure the highest number or, alternatively, sell it as is. I chose the former, which would be my biggest mistake, in hindsight.

Mired in the overwhelming day-to-day activities, I was prevented from fully embracing the new task at hand of identifying what areas needed new life breathed into them and getting the right people in the right seats to make the enhancements. The most glaring area in retrospect, which eluded me, was the product. So, time marched on, waiting for no one, and little changed.

Finding ourselves unable to replicate the massive success of 2013, our volume was sliding each year. It's hard to sell a company that isn't growing. If there was any hope of being acquired, what we needed but didn't have was a rock-solid plan to mitigate lagging sales coupled with a detailed, actionable roadmap for future success.

Furthermore, online sales were severely impacting the success of the stores because everyone had access, and the local retailers were no longer the only place to shop. Many just couldn't sustain themselves.

Randy, my Southeast rep, told me that if a store closed in an area or just stopped carrying the line, there was no one to replace the lost business. Social media further affected the retail landscape, influencing customers by opening their eyes to many more brands, hence more competition. Once a vibrant business model, selling the retailers became the land of diminishing returns.

Around this same time, a substantial blow came out of nowhere in my personal life, when my sister Maria, who was with me through it all, was suddenly diagnosed with bone cancer and died two months later. A small piece of me went with her that day, too. Losing my parents and even my much older brother was one thing. But, losing a sister, who I was extremely close with? That was another story. Believe me, we didn't always get along, but our love for one another was fierce and our bond unbreakable.

Maria, especially, was almost like a surrogate parent to me, being ten years older. She liked to buy me clothes and dress me up like a doll. I remember always fussing about when she did my hair. She taught me how to apply make-up. One of her tips was training our eyebrows to stay manicured by shaping and smoothing them with our fingertips daily.

She was whip smart and more compassionate than I ever was. She'd give you the shirt off her back. Any time I was in a quandary about anything, she'd have an answer.

She also taught me the many ways WD-40 can save the day when things are stuck. It makes me think of her and chuckle every time I reach for the WD to this day, which is often. I still miss her terribly, and when things were getting tougher with A&T, I wished I could simply pick up the phone to call her.

Though none as significant as losing a sibling, many more changes were on the horizon as the years passed. I knew the fashion tides were turning, too. This was made crystal clear when my Lucy's buyers said our holiday collection didn't retail because their shoppers were wearing lululemon to their New Year's Eve parties.

I thought, Ugh, what? Oh that sounds hot and sexy, like New Year's Eve. Not. First athleisure, and on its heels came normcore. Both trends that were too far left from what we were known for. It just felt like the hits kept coming.

Feeling I needed answers, my sales director, Nichole, and I did a tour of the Southeast territory. Through the years, the bulk of our A&T business had always come from there, and I wanted to see for myself all the stores we were selling or had sold previously to gain a better understanding of what was happening in the market.

I had the opportunity to see boutiques that I had been selling since my Times Two days. Some had been my customers for almost thirty years. My mind was blown and my eyes opened wide when I saw these stores with their product mixes and how we were positioned. Talking to the owners and their managers provided more valuable insights.

Whether it was the stores we were still selling or our former ride or die customers we visited, it was evident that we had been sticking to an old playbook when the game had changed. The trip only further reinforced the lack of trust I had in my abilities to give them what they needed or wanted. I felt I had lost my connection with who they even were. It was then that I really felt our fall from relevance.

Resort shoot in Rockaway Beach

The Rearview Mirror

ooking back, it's crystal clear that I had strayed from everything I learned and knew to be true. I stopped innovating. It's that simple. My whole career's success was built on spotting and exploiting the next emerging trend. The only constant thing in fashion is change. Somehow, in my relentless hustle and blind pursuit of success, I forgot that along the way.

As an entrepreneur, a creative one at that, you can't work in a silo with your head down, immersed in the minutiae of the day-to-day. I was involved in certain company activities that I had no business focusing on, and failing to empower members of my team meant everything came across my desk to get my stamp of approval. My office became a revolving door of people asking me questions all day long.

As a result, it was hard to focus on the actions I needed to take to uncover opportunities that could really move the company forward, namely, getting out of my office and traveling even more. Gregg, my GM, would say I always came back from my trips with exciting and innovative ideas. I credit this not only to the stimulation of what I encountered but also, by just leaving the HQ, my mind opened up like a sponge, absorbing new ideas and concepts.

Like my mentor Michael E. Gerber says, most entrepreneurs with small businesses find themselves as operators, not owners. In many cases, they simply create a lucrative job for themselves while remaining a slave to their business, working in it and not on it. Hand raised here.

I knew this truth after reading his first book decades earlier. I'd even spout it off as a warning to others while failing to heed the wise advice myself. For me, well, I was engaged in doing the very opposite, totally immersed in the daily grind of the business, neglecting to focus on the overall strategic vision, and feeling less and less passionate about it.

By that point, I'd grown accustomed to moseying around the trade shows, eyeing those other OGs I could commiserate with on the state of fashion. The system was broken and had been for a long time. We were in the segment of an industry, like so many others, that was severely impacted by production moving overseas and dramatic changes brought on by the internet and social media.

The mantra, "I'm working harder to make less money." usually meandered its way into the conversation. Unbeknownst to me at the time, while this was true, like many who had come up at the same time as me (those that were left, that is), I fell prey to living in a story, and a bleak one at that.

It's true that with fewer and fewer stores to sell, it was

far from the vibrant and emerging wholesale business model that held so much promise in the beginning of my career. I remember feeling sad for those who were just getting into the industry. They'd never experience the real fashion heyday when everything was fast-moving and buzzy, the way it was when I started.

But, looking back, it was all a state of mind. There was still excitement in lots of new ways that I was no longer a part of or privy to, existing in my own gloomy bubble.

I found myself living in an odd dichotomy. While my business was losing momentum with diminishing sales, my lifestyle hadn't changed since my income was still sufficient to maintain it. So, on the surface, everything seemed perfect. But, internally I was struggling and fearful for the future of the brand. With my ego fractured and an inner coping mechanism that drove me to push harder, I kept the train moving like I always did.

All the while, I knew in my heart of hearts that I wanted off the fashion merry-go-round. Five huge seasonal collections a year and a big team. Overdevelopment of product. Ever-changing and shrinking customer base. Differing opinions about what the brand should be from my US reps and my European distributor. It wasn't fun anymore.

I had grown numb to the excitement of opening a new account. It just felt like Groundhog Day. And I was starting to feel worn by the long, hard-working years of never letting up on the pedal. I had been working non-stop since I was a teenager, for God's sake. I was burnt out and didn't even know it.

Resort shoot on Shelter Island

It Takes a Village

All the writing was on the wall as it became increasingly difficult to think outside the box to grow the business. It just felt like trying to fix a car while driving it, impossible. With the industry's dramatic changes, our shrinking account base and working capital, a DTC channel that was fledgling in comparison, and my depleting energy and enthusiasm, I really felt I needed to stop the madness entirely and regroup.

Gregg and I floated the notion of not selling wholesale anymore and going all in on DTC. But, we'd have to restructure the whole company and take the leap into an unknown ocean. I was feeling pulled apart and out of control. Not a good place to be for a leader. And I repeat, I was not having fun.

I intuitively knew my design team wasn't up for the task at hand, either, though well-meaning and hardworking. I'd give them an initial design direction conceptually and expect them to run with it. Maybe I wasn't articulating our needs clearly enough. I've always just known a good number when I've seen it, so expressing what I had envisioned was admittedly a challenge toward the end.

Back and forth they'd go from my office to their work stations, I'm sure deflated because I demanded a lot. I wanted to see the future, and they were bringing me subtle variations on the product already out there. I would think, Can't someone have an original idea? I was frustrated. And even though I had a team, I felt alone.

Synergy is crucial, being able to groove together toward a common goal. I'd had those prolific designers on my team. Josandra is one. Coming from good fashion stock, her mom being a lingerie designer and professor at FIT, she had the ability to put together well thought out groups.

She'd create mood boards with flat sketches, illustrations, swatches, trims, and a couple of tear sheets. She clearly communicated a whole story. Easy to digest. Tweak a bit here and there, and, viola, a collection came to life. But, that creative groove was missing, and everyone on the team was feeling it. As was I.

And it wasn't just the team that was out of sync. Looking back, I can't say in all honesty that I was ever an Alice & Trixie girl through and through. I still had my downtown New York edge, which rarely coincided with the things we made anymore. That, too, put me in a bit of a dilemma as the years went by and the customer base evolved. Truth be told, I wanted to be designing different things and was unhappy creatively.

By the end of 2017, the year Ed Sheeran's "Shape of

You" soared to the top of the charts, we were still heading in the opposite direction, and it was completely evident that the synergy we badly needed had been replaced by discord. My own frustration and discontentment radiated, and everyone was feeling it, from design to sales. And my once steadfast confidence gave way to disheartening uncertainty. Something had to give.

While in Miami for a trade show, I was on a call with Randy, sharing my own realization that we were in dire need of changing things up. Standing in front of the Faena Hotel, I recall him saying, in no uncertain terms, that he felt we needed a total rebrand.

It felt like a bit of a punch at the time. When I said "change things up" I just meant take design in a new direction. But, I inherently knew he was right. And, it actually sounded great in theory. I would have the chance to express myself creatively in ways I felt I couldn't up to that point.

Though, rebranding is not easy. Among many other things, it involves changing your whole visual identity of logo, colors, fonts. Updating your website and all customer touch points. Altering the brand voice, repositioning the product, the list goes on. It's a costly endeavor, and after losing customers that liked you the way you were, it can take time and cost to acquire new ones. It's a step back to hopefully take two steps forward with nothing guaranteed. In light of everything, I just didn't feel up to the challenge of rallying myself and the troops to embark on a total rebrand.

After we hung up, I wandered into the decadent lobby of the hotel, aimlessly roaming toward the famed Damien

Hirst gilded dinosaur sculpture in their garden. Like a movie, my career flashed through my mind. Every line I ever bought, every designer I ever guided, every trade show and every market week I ever worked, every collection we pumped out, every inspo trip I took, every other move I made over all those decades, it all came crashing down on me.

The Only Way Out
Is Through

Cut to 2019. Lady Gaga and Bradley Cooper rocked the Oscars, singing mega hit "Shallow," and we designed our last collection, though we didn't know it at the time. Wooo, hold that thought.

Let's back up to 2018, the year Beyoncé made history, headlining Coachella. After returning from Miami, I did what I had always done and continued to persevere, though something was different. My eyes were opening wider, and I could no longer continue to bump along aimlessly at the bottom of my craft, or so it felt. Where were all my mentors when I needed them?

In my quest for guidance and ways to get myself and Alice & Trixie back on track, I first sought the advice of entrepreneurs in my circle. One such person, Rochelle, painted a foreboding picture when she told me of her experience investing another million dollars into her long-standing, struggling business only to wind up shutting it all down a year or two later. This notion scared the shit out of me.

I'd never borrowed a dime or added a penny to the original 150K I started A&T with, and I wanted to keep it that way. So, I made the firm decision that I would not use my hard-earned savings to reinvest. Amidst all the uncertainty, though, I continued going back and forth between ruminating about the future of the business and living in the moment, doing my best to carry on day-to-day.

Around this time, I ran into my neighbor, Ruth, who I hadn't seen in over a year. She was raving about a personal development seminar she was about to attend. Knowing I needed something to shift my perspective and being willing to try anything to get out of my funk, I thought, Why not? I'm in.

Inspired by Ruth's excitement that day, I would spend a year and a half attending a number of personal growth and professional business conferences. Even though I'd been in an industry for what seemed like forever, I learned about so much more that had eluded me while I had my head down, working diligently in my corner office for all those years.

My mind was opened up. I felt like a computer that was rebooted after being on for way too long, free from bugginess, running faster and smoother. I gained more clarity, and I felt empowered to turn Alice & Trixie around.

With my newfound resolve and enthusiasm, I went to yet another intensive business conference in Amsterdam. It was the kind of event where entrepreneurs and founders do deep dives into their organizations and learn about all the latest insights and intelligence from various industry thought leaders.

On this occasion, I had the rare opportunity to go over my numbers with one of these experts, named Keith. I shared the last five years of financials, and he was able to see the downward slope we were on. He looked at me with his empathic, hazy, blue eyes and said, "I think you know what you have to do."

As I went through the motions, completing the week at the conference, the reality of my situation slowly settled in and thoughts of "too little too late" began to consume me. With my financial cushion rapidly diminishing for the first time in all my years in business, I came to the stunning realization that I simply couldn't turn the ship around without more capital investment.

Knowing of Rochelle's ominous tale and taking to heart the advice I had just gotten as a definitive sign, protecting the wealth I built became mission critical. Although my primary focus for being there was to pick up the tools to get A&T back on track and save my business, I found I actually needed to save myself. So, as my conference peers readied themselves to go home and crush their businesses with all of their newfound awareness and education, I made the not-so-difficult decision to take a break.

Having allowed myself to take in Keith's clear-sighted perspective, I felt like I was suddenly let off the hook. He gave me license to stop pushing so hard. It was almost a relief, like part of me had been waiting for someone to give me permission to get off the merry-go-round.

When the event ended, I had plans to fly to Copenhagen for a shopping trip. It was a beautiful June day with the sun shining down upon me. Seated with my latte at an outdoor cafe, I started wondering, What the hell am I doing in Copenhagen? My next thought raced to how I needed to go home and break the news that Alice & Trixie would be closing... at least for now.

As fate would have it, I then glanced to my right and there, seated next to me, was an attractive, cool-looking guy in his thirties. We got to talking, and it turned out that he was a fashion photographer by the name of Simon. Not French, if you were wondering. Our conversation was natural and easy, and I found myself sharing about my experience in Amsterdam.

Aside from fashion, we had a lot in common as we chatted about our personal development journeys. He was delighted to share how the Pomodoro Technique was helping him get more done. And I turned him on to doing his first Instagram Live, which we did together to commemorate the milestone.

The next day, he took me bicycling all through colorful, picture-perfect Copenhagen, and we ended up at Reffen. A sprawling outdoor venue whose ethos is sustainability, it had dozens of stalls serving a diverse array of authentic bold-flavored street foods from near and far. From Cajun grilled oysters to Argentinian empanadas and Kurdish kebabs, they had it all.

We walked around and sat on the waterfront chatting as we indulged ourselves in these tasty delights. With the day's adventures a warm and welcome distraction from the broader reality of what was looming, I felt grateful for the respite.

The following day, I slipped into my usual travel mode and shopped the stores alone, although with less zeal than I otherwise would have had. I was simply doing what was routine. When in Rome.

Feeling sluggish, I regretfully skipped the Louisiana Museum of Modern Art before taking myself to dinner that night. In between bites of my rare black peppercorn steak, I began to contemplate the discussions in my head that I'd have when I got back to New York. The reality that this was actually happening started settling into my mind.

On the Friday that I was leaving, my newfound friend invited me to join him for a meet-up geared toward creatives, which was new to me even though it was a global organization founded in New York. After buttery croissants, coffee and an inspiring talk, I actually felt slightly optimistic and hopeful as I ended my time in Copenhagen.

Holiday shoot in my Soho loft

It's a Wrap

pon my return home, I called Gregg into my office to share my intentions. I don't think he saw it coming, although he didn't seem entirely surprised. We then broke the news to everyone on the team that we would be winding down the operation. Now, they were all surprised, but they seemingly understood. The crew dismantled slowly over four jam-packed months as we got everything in order.

There were a lot of moving parts and things to be addressed in the process. Anything that would produce revenue was tackled first and foremost. Producing and shipping orders for the current season was of the highest priority. Selling off the inventory we had hanging. Selling off excess fabric in-house and at Ma's cutting room. Selling off the valuable vintage collection we amassed over two decades. Selling our office furniture, cutting tables, Juki sewing machines, and mannequins along with the rest.

The HQ had acquired so much over the course of the last fifteen years. Sample yardage and every conceivable trim, hard patterns, soft patterns, markers, design room supplies, office supplies, kitchen supplies, signage and trade show furnishings, hangers and rolling racks. The list goes on. One massive purge. What could fetch a buck got sold, and other things were discarded or donated.

I met many young designers and brands looking to pick up second hand goods as we cleared everything out. Among those who needed design-related things like cutting tables, sewing machines and mannequins, one such brand came for a couple of file cabinets. Previously a tech founder, this man had an idea to manufacture terry cloth rowing jackets that he sold to high-end hotels and resorts. Our white wooden hangers went to a fashiony cool-kid from Brooklyn who upcycled vintage.

In this process of unraveling what we'd built over so many years, I spoke with many of my building neighbors, some for the first time, who were lured in by the conspicuous for sale signs we placed throughout. It was refreshing to see that while we were winding down, so many others were ramping up. It was an interesting time that began to open my eyes to the fact that fashion was still very much alive and well in New York City.

The things we ultimately kept were the intellectual property of Alice & Trixie. Design archive samples, design binders with silhouettes and seasonal collections, our vast print library of strike-offs, custom color swatch library of every hue we ever did, and then some. Patterns were all kept digitally, so we discarded the physical ones. Still, it broke my heart to see them all bent and stuffed into dumpsters.

Even so, I remember feeling like a weight was being

lifted, and a newfound sense of freedom settled in with each passing day. The emptiness of the space in the final days brought an overwhelming sense of buoyancy. Everything was going as planned and falling into place like a precision game of Tetris under my methodical supervision. With all the loose ends tied up, we finally closed up shop in October 2019 to revamp and reboot, or so I thought.

Knowing I needed to make significant changes and not wanting to throw in the towel completely, I kept my New York City HQ by renting out a portion of it. Even after the final team members left for the last time, I still found myself going into the office and sitting at my desk. I had a deeply ingrained routine that was hard to break, even though there was no longer any business to transact.

So, I found other uses for my office. I was invited to mentor a young brand in the FIT Design Entrepreneurs program, and I routinely met with them there. At the same time, I decided to start a YouTube channel to provide educational content. So, I'd have meetings with my new intern/videographer there, too.

I wasn't really sure where everything was headed. But, without the daily stresses of running a company, I was spreading my wings for the first time in a long time, doing what I wanted, whenever I wanted, kind of like when I started Times Two. It was liberating, and the world was my oyster again.

After three months, I decided to hit the West Coast and see if I might realize my life-long dream of becoming bi-coastal. Maybe restart Alice & Trixie there. My plan was to begin up north and take the scenic Highway 1 down to

Los Angeles, where I'd visit with friends and start looking for a place.

I had every intention of coming back to business after a well-deserved hiatus, maybe six months. But, someone upstairs had a different plan. The day before I was scheduled to fly out west, New York had its first lockdown. With my bags already packed, I scooped up my little chihuahua mix, Chloé, and drove east to my place in the Hamptons.

Just when I was settling into a normal-paced life for the first time in literally decades and contemplating what would be next on my adventure, COVID arrived and forced me to disconnect from all things business. Not the excursion I had envisioned.

Illusion of Confusion

y home felt like a quiet oasis amidst all the chaos going on around the globe, especially in NYC, which got hit the hardest in the beginning. Remembering ominous news flashes of refrigerated trucks waiting to take away the deceased still gives me chills. I decided to turn off the news to preserve my sanity, and instead took to the internet with everyone else on the planet, learning all sorts of things that I otherwise never had time for.

I consumed copious amounts of content in the way of books, podcasts, virtual seminars and bootcamps. I completed several online courses. All in an effort to figure out what I wanted to be when I grew up. Only, I was a grown-ass woman having these thoughts.

My mind was buzzing with new ideas. Thoughts of relaunching were replaced by the existential question, What else can I do in a lifetime? It was a time of soul-searching, deep reflection and, along with it, renewal.

In retrospect, there were many fits and starts, similar

to when I was younger. Along with the rest of the world it seemed, I thought about starting a podcast. Then, it was a blog or creating a fashion course. I recorded my first podcast episode, I built a website with a blog, and I outlined a complete fashion curriculum. But, I'd get part way through and the initial excitement about each one was short-lived and just fizzled out, which led me to abandon ship on every last one of these concepts.

As an entrepreneur, I've always fancied myself an idea person. But, a concept without conviction and execution is just a wasted thought. So, finding myself with an onslaught of ideas about what I could do and lacking a steady commitment was overwhelming to say the least. Much of the time, this left me feeling disappointed and lost, unclear about what my goals were anymore. How did I get here?

I wondered why I was so indecisive, not possessing the mental stamina to see things through. This harkened back to the time in my youth when I lacked consistency, trying so many different things. I couldn't articulate it as a teen, but I was actually searching for my bliss, my purpose. Finding and choosing my own adventure. And decades later, the same was true.

I'd ask myself, What's different now than when I started Times Two in 1989? As I looked back, it all seemed so easy. There were no questions to answer, no apprehensions.

The lightbulb moment finally came when I realized that back then I had my eye on the prize. One prize, one course of action. Blinders on, focused. Upon this revelation, I coined the phrase, "Dabblers don't dominate." Ok, so one course of action. But, which one?

My friend Seth once told me that in sports, sometimes, the players have to let the ball just come to them. To the contrary, my whole life and career had been about driving my success and making shit happen, never waiting for anything to come to me. I finally realized I had to stop thinking, tirelessly trying to figure it out.

Throughout my success, I had never had it all figured out, anyway. As I look back, connecting the dots, I imagine all the angels that swirled around me through the years and recall the messages I received at various intervals that prepared me for things to come. The Candys and the Steves of the world. Even Dr. Jekyll and Mr. Hyde. The people that greatly impacted me in such subtle ways and propelled me forward. I've always been divinely guided. I believe we all are, in fact, if we take notice

My mind had been spinning with questions. I needed to turn it all off and just be. Breathe. Let go. Surrender to the flow of the lazy river gently guiding me to my destination. In doing so, the proverbial ball came to me in the form of writing this book.

As I look back, do I still wish I cashed out of Alice & Trixie with lots of fanfare and a glorious exit? Hell yeah. But, if I had a crystal ball, we'd be stretched out on loungers pondering one question, "Beach or pool today?" Though, in reality, I couldn't imagine doing that for very long.

I'm still filled with so much wonder and excitement and a burning desire that propels me forward. My journey is far from over, and the fashion industry has afforded me a life many would envy. No regrets.

Me as a hipster kid in my ringer
screen-printed tee, circa 1969

Endings are Beginnings in Disguise

ut to late 2022. "As It Was," the Harry Styles mega-hit, marked the longest reigning number one single by a solo act in Hot 100 history at fifteen weeks. Ironically, this track has a sound reminiscent of the late '80s, when I began my humble ride as an entrepreneur, and my reign has lasted over three decades.

The last few years have been a voyage of self-discovery and resilience. I still don't have all the answers and probably never will. But, the one thing that has become abundantly clear is that sometimes you have to leave to come home again.

At my core, I'm still that same young girl from the Five Towns who couldn't scramble home fast enough to put on her first pair of hot pants and who had big dreams of doing something spectacular with her life as she marched across that fireplace hearth and through the streets of New York City. And all these years later, after three killer decades of success, with one ending came a new beginning. Life pushed me once again out of my comfort zone to explore new things that challenged me and helped me grow, as is often the case when things don't go according to our best-laid plans.

Although, if I could, I'd have written my life's story differently. In it, I'd be able to call my mom and tell her I was doing a new thing. She'd pause, of course, and I'd smile, and enthusiastically tell her I'd written a book. She'd be the first one to read it and tell me how proud she was. This I know for sure. And I'd have had more time with my dad to get to know one another better and to learn more about how he left his homeland, persevered and made it as an entrepreneur. And my big brother and big sister would still be here to share good times with.

But, despite all the heartache I've felt over the losses in my life and the rigorous demands I placed on myself for fear that if I slowed down, I'd be crushed by that Indiana Jones boulder, still, fashion was always the place I felt most at home, almost like it's a part of my DNA. I planted my flag there all those years ago and now, with a deeper understanding of myself and my place in the world and a newfound appreciation and outlook, I've made my way back to where I have always truly belonged.

There really is no place like home. It's a place where I can further explore my creativity in new ways, recognizing that any limitations that may exist are of my own making and don't serve me. Of course it's difficult to let go of what once was, the way things were. And there are things I will always miss about the hustle and grind of New York's fashion district that I relished for so many years.

But, today is all any one of us really has and the present has its riches if we choose to take notice and live in the moment, embracing any changes that may come our way. For I've learned that change is the one constant in life. And now, answering that existential question of what else I could do in a lifetime, well, just about anything I set my mind to. The prize is always there for the taking should we dare to pursue our dreams.

This has been my love letter to my beloved industry. I wrote it not only to highlight and preserve the rich history of New York City's fashion district but to hopefully inspire and guide you by sharing my well-worn experiences.

For all of you emerging superstars, aiming sky-high in the pursuit of making your mark, I hope you culled the lessons embedded within my story and that you will summon the requisite drive and audacity to carve out your space in this aspirational and fascinating industry.

For those of you reading just for fun, wanting to catch a sneak peek of what goes on behind those coveted doors and break through the mystique that shrouds the fashion industry, I hope my story has broadened your perspective and encouraged you to pursue the things that will make your heart sing.

Whoever you are, whatever you do, just crush it! And remember: Dabblers don't dominate.

As for me, well, I'm a fellow traveler on the journey who still sees the world as a playground for my imagination, forever exploring new ways to tap into my creativity and push my boundaries. Staying curious and engaged, my eyes always open as I scope out fresh experiences and opportunities to learn and grow, forever on the hunt for what's next.

The ~~End~~
Beginning...

Acknowledgements

No bucket list item. No someday, maybe. Never setting out to write a book, here I find myself. So, I feel obliged and delighted to acknowledge the milestones and the people that brought me to this point.

First and foremost, I would like to extend my deepest thanks to my family, who instilled in me the belief that valuable accomplishments often demand fierce determination and hard work. And most importantly that I was capable of achieving whatever I put my mind to.

I would like to thank my earliest business mentors, Freddy and Albert Attias, and Soly and Albert Safdieh. The foundation that was to become my springboard to success was laid in place by them. Without their extraordinary powers of example and belief in me, I don't know how my career trajectory would have played out.

I would like to thank Paul Davison and Rohan Seth, the founders of social audio app Clubhouse and Imran Ahmed, the BOF founder, who welcomed me into the universe of their invite-only app during the lockdowns of 2020. In a time when most people's lives were shrinking, mine was expanding. Without them I would have never met the people from all over the globe that impacted me: one who sparked the notion that I might write a book and several who inspired me along my writing journey.

I'd like to thank John Andrade, who told me he was writing a book. And if you read the previous pages, you'll know my MO, so it got me thinking: If John can do it, so can I. And so it began.

I'd like to thank my friend, published author and marketer Antonio White, who kept cheering me on, so much so that I sent him an initial rough draft of the manuscript to read, a non-fiction how-to book for entrepreneurs. Taking his no-holds-barred feedback into consideration, I chose to delete two-thirds of the book and go back to writing my story, this memoir. I still remember his words echoing, "I don't want to know how to do it, I want to know how you did it."

I'd like to thank the vibrant writer community on Clubhouse, which opens its arms and minds to new authors. I learned so much. I want to express my gratitude to the publishing and marketing podcasters and their guests that share their insights. I remain a sponge, absorbing your knowledge and wisdom. I always found myself magically in the right place at the right time, hearing the exact words that would propel me forward in that moment.

I'd like to thank all of my dedicated team members and sales reps who were with me through the years and invested themselves in the success of Times Two and Alice & Trixie. It's in hindsight that I see I wasn't vocal enough signaling my appreciation for your hard work and efforts. You were all part of the fabric of my journey and without that this story wouldn't have a reason to be.

For the same reason, I'd like to thank Mr. Ma, my bulk cutter, who cut my first pattern and my last at Alice & Trixie. I'd also like to thank Verna and Louie, proprietors of my main factory who busted their asses to deliver on time, which they did, and John and Alex from Accurate Patterns who saved me a lot of fabric and money from the beginning making those tight markers.

I'd like to thank Steve from Parasuco who made a profound impact on my life the day he said, "Take the showroom, you'll get a line." His simple, yet powerful words instilled in me the confidence to move forward and fueled my journey, unbeknownst to him. Without them, this book would not have been possible all these years later.

I'd like to thank Denny and Judy for taking a shot on this newbie and placing their faith and trust in me to nurture and grow their business. Who would've known back then that their influence could have played a pivotal role in paving the way for the success I can write about now.

I'd like to thank my trusted friend, Bryan Davis, for being a solid sounding board, reading several drafts and offering invaluable feedback all along the way. Whether he was in Egypt or Africa or Thailand he was there for me.

I'd like to thank Hanna Day-Tenerowicz, my book designer. Feeling in sync from the start, her sparkling creativity and positive energy made her a wonderful collaborator for this project.

Thanks to Dorothy Andreas, who introduced me to Alissa Ellett, my ride-or-die editor. An exceptional collaborator, Alissa taught me so much in this process and has made me a better writer. I'm forever grateful.

Lastly, I want to express my heartfelt gratitude to every person and every experience that played a part in shaping the path that led to the publishing of this memoir.

Angela Taylor George

Angela Taylor George, founder of trend-setting, multi-brand showroom Times Two and renowned New York label Alice & Trixie, is an entrepreneur, fashion designer, creative director and author.

Hailed early on as the Voice of Authority by New York Daily News, Angela has made an indelible mark on fashion internationally over four decades, playing a vital role in the co-creation and launch of major fashion trends widely copied today and originating designs still cherished and traded around the world.

When not in pursuit of the next big fashion trend, she's designing interiors, snapping artsy pics with her trusty iPhone, and, of course, ever eyeing her next travel destination.

Angela resides in New York City and East Hampton, New York with her adorable rescue pup, Chloe.

www.angelataylorgeorge.com

Scan the code and never miss a beat! xx